THE CATAMARAN BOOK

CATAMARAN SAILING FROM **START TO FINISH**

START TO FINISH
CLASS GUIDES

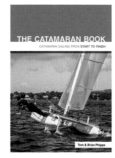

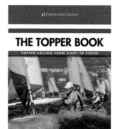

From beginner to serious racer, get the most out of your chosen vessel with the **Start to Finish** series.

Find out more at **www.fernhurstbooks.com**

THE CATAMARAN BOOK

CATAMARAN SAILING FROM **START TO FINISH**

Tom & Brian Phipps

FERNHURST
BOOKS

Reprinted in 2022 by Fernhurst Books Limited
Published in 2017 by Fernhurst Books Limited

The Windmill, Mill Lane, Harbury, Leamington Spa, Warwickshire. CV33 9HP. UK
Tel: +44 (0) 1926 337488 | www.fernhurstbooks.com

A catalogue record for this book is available from the British Library
ISBN 978-1-909911-57-4

The authors and publisher would like to express their considerable thanks to Rupert White and Robyn Curnow for taking part in the photoshoots. The publisher would like to thank those who have helped source and supply photographs for this book. Every effort has been made to contact the relevant copyright holders and any errors or ommissions have been made unknowingly.

Front cover photograph © Tom Gruitt/Fernhurst Books Limited
Back cover photographs: left © RS Sailing; middle © Hobie Cat Europe; right © Brian Phipps; bottom © mycteria/Shutterstock

All photographs © Tom Gruitt/Fernhurst Books Limited
Except: p13, 21-32, 44-45, 50, 54 (top), 55, 60-61, 64, 66, 79 (top), 82-83, 85-87, 95 (bottom), 100-101, 104-106, 119, 122-123, 124 (bottom), 127, 134 © Fernhurst Books Limited; p16 © Katherine Leather; p38 (right), 48 (top right) © Topper International; p48 (bottom right) © RS Sailing; p68 © LaserPerformance; p75, 136 © Hobie Cat Europe; p102, 150 © Brian Phipps; p125 © Champion Marine Photography; p137 © Geoff Gritton; p141 © Iain Philpott; p145 © Pinnell & Bax; p148 © Andy McRobbie; p149, 151 © James Avery; p152 © Helena Darvelid; p153 © Ricardo Rosario

Designed & typeset by Rachel Atkins
Illustrated by Maggie Nelson
Printed in Malta by Melita Press

TOM & BRIAN PHIPPS
CATAMARAN EXPERTS

Tom Phipps is a professional sailor, and has been sailing catamarans since the age of 10. He dominated catamaran racing at a youth level, medalling three times at the ISAF Youth World Championships and winning three times at the RYA Youth Nationals. From these promising beginnings Tom has gone on to win a number of national championships: the Dart, Formula 18, Hobie 16 (2x) and Tornado classes; succeeded in the Hobie 16, Formula 16 and Student Keelboat European championships; and claimed victory in the Dart World championships, two times over.

Tom has also competed in the C Class World Championships (often called the 'Little America's Cup') in a wing-sailed catamaran, raced in the Flying Phantom professional catamaran series and was a helm on the Extreme Sailing Series in the foiling GC32 catamaran. He sailed a Nacra 17 catamaran for two Olympic campaigns and narrowly missed the GBR team selection for the Rio 2016 Olympic Games.

He has now moved into more of a coaching and tuition role, heading up Windsport and Coastland at the family's training base in Cornwall.

Brian Phipps, Tom's father, has been involved in manufacturing, sailing and racing catamarans since 1978. He has won various catamaran championships in his time and now supplies a range of catamarans, coaching and technical support worldwide.

He set up the Windsport Cat Clinics that provide an ideal introduction to the practical business of catamaran sailing delivering basic skills and performance coaching to sailing teams all over the world. He was the RYA Catamaran Youth Coach and has coached in the UK, China, Dubai, Ireland, Jersey and Oman.

CONTENTS

FOREWORD
BY SANTIAGO LANGE

Catamaran sailing is an incredible sport, and one that can have you hooked for life. I started cat sailing back in 1997, transferring from the Laser, and have been lucky enough to represent Argentina in seven Olympic Games, winning two bronze medals in the Tornado class. I was thrilled to win gold in the Nacra 17 at Rio 2016, aged 54, and follow that up by sailing in the Tokyo 2020 Olympics.

Catamaran sailing is a lifetime sport, largely because it is great fun – whether you are sailing a beach cat on a sailing holiday, racing at your local club, competing nationally or internationally, aiming for the Olympics or even having a tilt at the America's Cup. The stable platform and turn of speed provided by the two hulls will put a smile on anyone's face!

But to get the most out of your catamaran sailing you absolutely have to get the basics right, and that is where this book comes in. Tom and Brian Phipps, who have also spent their lifetimes devoted to catamaran sailing, provide an indispensable, solid foundation which takes you from your first trip on board a cat to competing at a serious level.

Tom Phipps lit up the catamaran youth sailing world from 2004 with his amazing successes at the ISAF (now World Sailing) Youth Championships – medalling 3 years in a row, two of them gold. He competed on the Olympic circuit and certainly knows what he is talking about. I have enjoyed racing against Tom (even if sometimes I wish he wasn't quite so talented!).

Just like me, Tom has been inspired and influenced throughout his sailing career by his father. Brian Phipps has been at the centre of catamaran sailing in the UK, and elsewhere, for many decades and has had success in an enviable list of catamaran championships in his time.

This tremendous book presents both Tom and Brian's enormous knowledge of catamaran sailing, and the industry as a whole, as well as conveying their passion for and dedication to the sport.

If you want to enjoy catamaran sailing, and improve your skills, I thoroughly recommend this book.

Good luck, and I hope to see you out on the water!

Santiago Lange
Nacra 17 gold medallist, Rio Olympic Games, 2016
World Sailing's Sailor of the Year, 2016
7-time Olympian: 1 x gold, 2 x bronze

INTRODUCTION

Why is sailing catamarans so very special? Is it their speed? Is it their power? Is it their shape? Is it their size? By the time you have finished using this book we hope that we will have contributed to your catamaran knowledge and your future enjoyment of this fast-moving and exciting discipline of sailing. The book is arranged into four parts providing support and knowledge from your first experience through to glimpses of the latest developments in cat sailing.

Your hosts, Tom Phipps, international catamaran racer, and Brian Phipps, specialist catamaran trainer / coach, have brought together all their training, coaching and catamaran racing techniques, skills and knowledge to provide something that every developing catamaran sailor can draw on.

To new cat sailors: welcome. Catamarans are fast and fun; we encourage you to aim high and enjoy your catamaran sailing as much as – and maybe even more than – we have, and still do. Catamaran sailing is a discipline just like sailing dinghies, windsurfers and keelboats; the earlier you start, and the more time you spend on the water, the better you become. So aim high and make your mark on the sport of sailing by sailing a catamaran.

Part One introduces the total novice to the very basics: the catamaran platform, rig and how to use the wind through to enjoying your first sail, explaining all aspects of catamaran sailing in wind forces 2 and 3. Experienced sailors from other sailing disciplines may wish to browse through this section, noting the subtle differences they should be aware of when moving to catamarans.

Part Two contains information for those who can already sail other types of craft and those who have successfully completed Part One, focussing on 'standard' catamarans like the Dart, Nacra and Hobie ranges. It covers light and strong wind techniques, trapezing, downwind sailing and sailing on the sea. You will gain an insight into handling your cat in adverse conditions so that, when you are out sailing in stronger winds, the potential speed will be thrilling not frightening, and light winds rewarding rather than frustrating.

An introduction to the main aspects of racing is also included, with the emphasis on how to get the best out of your cat and improve your position in a race – perfect as the introduction to club racing and local regattas. Catamarans are fast, situations change rapidly and advantages can be won and lost quickly, so you must try to stay on top of each situation in order to achieve your best result.

Part Three covers the more advanced – high performance – catamarans, and the challenges and knowledge required to master them over and above what has already been covered. Many cats are fitted with a gennaker (an asymmetric spinnaker), and we look in detail at how to handle these exciting downwind sails. To counteract the extra power generated there is the double trapezing option so helming from the wire and advanced techniques in the race environment are also covered.

Part Four introduces some of the exciting current developments in our sport. Foiling and wing sails are looked at through Tom's personal experiences of both racing and being involved in their development.

Whatever your catamaran experience: welcome. We have three things in common:

- **Speed**
- **Power**
- **Two Hulls**

We look forward to seeing you on the water!

PART 1
GETTING STARTED

There is a wide range of catamarans varying in hull shape, sail plan, number in the crew, complexity and performance. Some have centreboards, others daggerboards, while others have skegs or even asymmetric hulls. Whichever type you choose, the basic sailing techniques and concepts are the same; the important thing is that your cat provides the sort of sailing, fun and thrills you desire.

Don't just take the manufacturers' or owners' word for it – book a trial sail, talk to other catamaran sailors, find out about class associations, second-hand values, technical support, replacement parts and where you might sail. It is important that your cat fits your sailing needs as well as your pocket! There is limited benefit buying an all-out racing machine if you simply want to cruise or race at your local club with a strong fleet of another catamaran class.

Capsizing and tacking a catamaran are often the biggest concerns for the beginner. A well-designed catamaran is easily righted, tacked and manoeuvred using the correct techniques; so just like anything else you plan to buy: take reliable advice, have a sail and you will not be disappointed.

HULL SHAPE

The choice of hull shape depends on your sailing requirements. Almost all shapes will perform adequately in a range of conditions, but excel in only a few. The higher the performance, the greater the need for protective care, regular maintenance, and attention to the hull's skin.

HULLS WITH SKEGS

Each hull is identical in shape, and sideways movement through the water is restricted by a deep keel that forms a skeg about two-thirds of the way along the hull.

Well suited to both flat water and sea conditions, the skeg system is often seen in European-designed club fleet racing and leisure designs as it merges performance with simplicity.

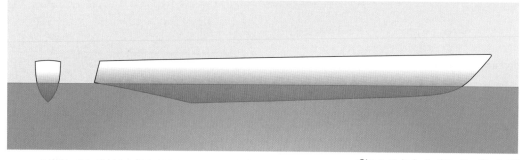

Skeg-style hulls (like the Dart 18)

ASYMMETRIC HULLS

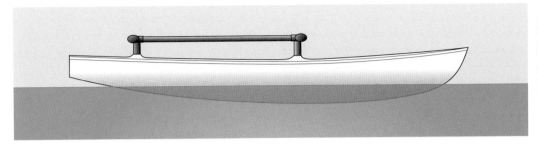

Asymmetric hulls are designed to replace dagger-boards or centreboards. Each hull is handed – that is to say that the port hull is a mirror image of the starboard hull. Although not as efficient as hulls with boards, asymmetric hulls do simplify the layout of the catamaran, making it simpler to handle and maintain.

The amount of rocker (curve) built into the hull shape can affect handling: more rocker can lead to less stability fore and aft.

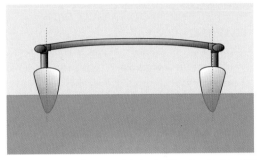

Asymmetric hulls (like the Hobie 16)

HULL WITH CENTREBOARDS / DAGGERBOARDS

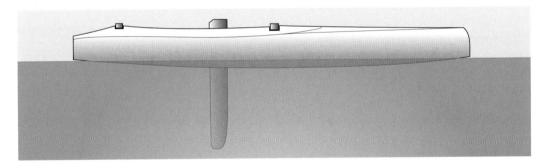

Catamarans fitted with daggerboards or centre-boards are generally the most efficient upwind per-formers. They do, however, require maintenance, and must be handled carefully when launching and beaching. Avoid underwater obstructions to prevent damage to the foils or the hull.

Centreboards fold up into a cassette inside the hull whilst daggerboards, when raised, protrude from the deck line. Either way, take care to prevent stones and sand getting into the boxed area when beaching, as this will restrict movement and can cause internal damage.

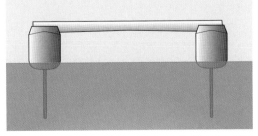

Hulls with daggerboards (like the F16)

Some daggerboards are now designed to give ver-tical lift (e.g. C-Foils and J-Foils). See Part 4.

HULL MATERIAL OPTIONS

WOOD COMPOSITES

Wood is an option for those who enjoy building a leisure or lightweight performance hull at home. Wood laminates and epoxy's can provide excellent strength to weight ratios but you are unlikely to find a modern production catamaran in this material. Older catamarans made using wood laminates should be inspected with care.

POLYPROPYLENE (ROTA-MOULDED) STYLE MATERIALS

This is the most popular material, in recent years, for training school-designed catamarans due to its durability and low cost of manufacture per unit. Rota moulded catamarans provide a robust hull platform that can take the knocks of sailing tuition and beach grounding, providing a low maintenance cat. These advantages are balanced by hull weight, stiffness and repair: all things that affect the practicality and how a catamaran handles and performs on and off the water.

GRP (FIBERGLASS)

GRP resins, materials and construction methods have progressed in all aspects since the early sixties. It is the most popular material for most class racing catamarans combining strength with lightness, durability with life span. Damage to a GRP hull can normally be repaired by an experienced technician to a standard that will not affect performance.

CARBON FIBRE LAMINATE

The cutting edge of catamaran manufacture: carbon fibre laminates provide the ultimate in strength, stiffness and lightness. Largely used on cats that are pushing the very edge of catamaran sailing boundaries, the cost of these craft reflect the various technologies involved.

SAIL PLAN

The vast majority of catamarans have fully battened mainsails and high-ratio jibs for maximum efficiency. The sail material can vary from Dacron to Mylar depending on the sail's design shape and function.

Some mainsails are supported along the foot by a boom; others are loose-footed, with no boom. A boom allows additional adjustment and control of the mainsail shape and rig tuning. A loose-footed sail simplifies the system and does away with the complication and restrictions of a boom, with the sail shape and position controlled by the mainsheet tension, traveller and sheeting angle.

NUMBER OF CREW

There is nothing quite like sailing a catamaran as a team, with helm and crew working together to get the maximum performance out of their cat. But the reality is that many people find it hard to get a regular crew. Fortunately there are plenty of catamarans for single-handed sailing.

The Shadow X is a high performance single-handed cat

The diagrams on pages 19 and 20 show you what most parts of your catamaran are called, but here are a few more words which it will be useful to know.

Aft	Towards the back of the cat
Block	A unit with a wheel inserted which ropes run through (pulley)
Bung	A drainage plug found on some hulls
Foils	Generally: those surfaces under the water that are retractable: rudders, centreboards, daggerboards; sometimes: hydrofoils that can raise the cat out of the water when sailing
Forward	Towards the front of a cat
Gudgeons	Fittings on the transom with a hole to secure the rudder
Halyard	A rope or wire used to hoist or lower sails
Leeward	The side of the cat on which the mainsail is set when sailing (away from the wind)
Pintles	Pin-like fittings on the rudder to secure the rudder to the gudgeons
Platform	The area the team move around on: the hulls and trampoline
Port	Left
Shackle	A 'U' shaped piece of metal secured with a pin, used for securing halyards to sails etc.
Sheave	A wheel in a block or pulley
Starboard	Right
Windward	The side of the cat opposite to which the mainsail is set when sailing (closer to the wind)

DETAILED DESCRIPTIONS

THE HULLS

Each hull is a sealed unit, with built-in buoyancy to keep it afloat if damaged. A small breather hole positioned in a suitable location above the water-line allows for changes in air pressure. All fittings attached to the hull are sealed to prevent water ingress.

MAINSAIL DOWNHAUL (TYPICALLY CALLED THE CUNNINGHAM IN A DINGHY)

The mainsail downhaul is a control system attached to the tack of the sail to help shape and provide power control. You will notice that with no tension on the luff (the front edge of the sail), the mainsail has little shape and is rather like a flat piece of cardboard. When the downhaul is tensioned the sail and mast are forced into a shape that changes the camber of the sail to produce the wing effect.

SPANNER LINE OR BAR

The spanner line or bar is normally connected to the foot of the mainsail or boom and to the bottom of the mast. It is adjusted to control the amount of mast rotation for the required airflow over the mainsail in relation to mast bend.

JIB & MAINSAIL HALYARDS

The halyards are the lines that hoist the sails. They are often part of a halyard lock system as described later in the book.

SHROUDS, FORESTAY & BRIDLE WIRES

These are the wires / lines that hold the mast upright (standing rigging). They are subjected to incredible stress and should be checked regularly for any sign of corrosion or wear as should their connections.

TRAPEZE WIRES

The purpose of a trapeze wire is to support the crew (or helmsman) when they extend their body weight outboard by 'standing' on the edge of the hull.

The wires are connected to the mast about two-thirds of the way up and run down almost parallel to the shrouds. They each have a large connecting ring at the bottom that clips into the crew's trapeze harness, and are loosely connected to the catamaran by shock-cord. They can be adjusted to support the crew at the correct trapeze height.

TRAPEZE RESTRAINING LINE

The restraining lines (if fitted) are connected to the transom of the cat and can be used in conjunction with the trapeze wire system to provide added stability when reaching in strong winds to prevent the crew from being pulled forward.

RUDDER & TILLER ASSEMBLY

The rudders are normally fixed in the raised position when on the beach and then lowered when the cat is on the water. The tiller arms are joined by a connecting bar controlled by the helm via the tiller extension. The tiller extension is your steering mechanism and you should hold it at all times when sailing.

MAINSHEET, JIBSHEET & TRAVELLER LINE

These are the ropes that control the positions of the sails. The helm and crew should be able to adjust these at any time to allow for changes in wind

strength or direction, just as you would do with the accelerator and brake pedals in a car.

TRAMPOLINE & TOESTRAPS

The trampoline covers the area between the hulls to allow easy movement from one hull to the other. The toestraps lie along the trampoline and secure your feet when you lean out over the side of the hull. As the crew or helm becomes more proficient, they will use the trapeze, and may use the foot-loops (if fitted) positioned along the side of the hull.

MAIN & REAR BEAMS

These are the spars that hold the two hulls together. There are various methods of attachment from sleeves in the hull to beam bolts and clamps. They must be securely fastened and in good condition along with the fixing attachments.

MAST & MAST BALL

The mast sits in the mast ball (attached to the main beam) allowing the mast to rotate about its axis, giving improved airflow over the sails. The mast itself is normally a sealed unit, giving a degree of buoyancy that helps reduce the possibility of a capsize inversion. It also aids capsize recovery should that occur.

DIAMOND WIRES & SPREADERS

These can be used to control the mast support and profile on higher performance catamarans. A combination of spreader angle and diamond tension creates pre-bend fore and aft as well as sideways support.

GENNAKER

Also referred to as an asymmetric spinnaker, this light weight sail is used largely to increase downwind performance. It is stored in a chute or similar when sailing upwind or not in use.

RIGHTING LINE

The righting line is your aid to righting your catamaran following a capsize. It is normally secured around the mast heel and stored in place where it can easily be retrieved.

STANDARD CAT

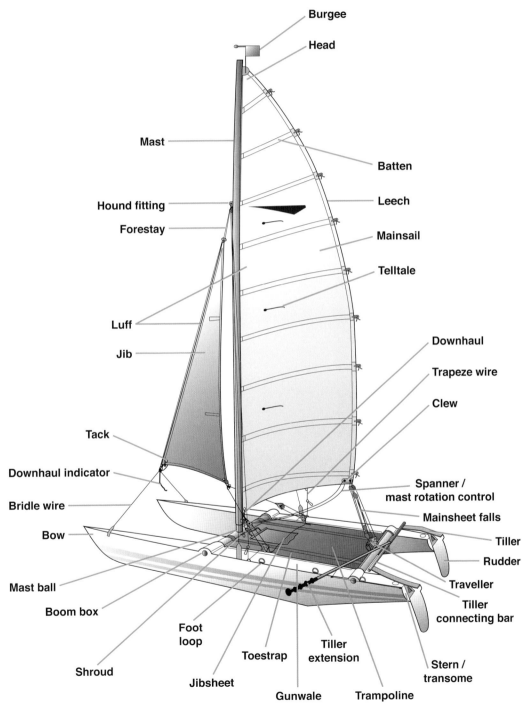

Burgee

Head

Mast

Batten

Leech

Hound fitting

Forestay

Mainsail

Telltale

Luff

Jib

Downhaul

Trapeze wire

Clew

Tack

Downhaul indicator

Bridle wire

Bow

Spanner / mast rotation control

Mainsheet falls

Tiller

Rudder

Mast ball

Traveller

Boom box

Tiller connecting bar

Foot loop

Toestrap

Tiller extension

Shroud

Stern / transome

Jibsheet

Gunwale

Trampoline

Dart 18 with parts labelled

HIGH PERFORMANCE CAT

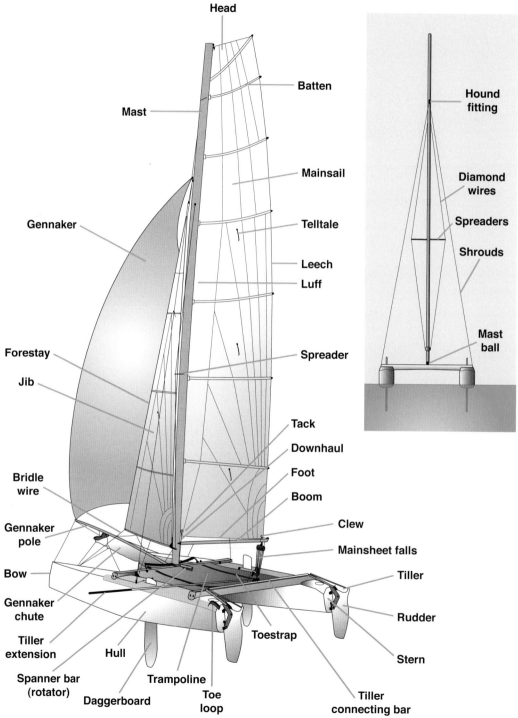

Head

Batten

Mast

Mainsail

Gennaker

Telltale

Leech

Luff

Forestay

Spreader

Jib

Tack

Downhaul

Foot

Bridle wire

Boom

Gennaker pole

Clew

Mainsheet falls

Bow

Tiller

Gennaker chute

Rudder

Tiller extension

Hull

Toestrap

Stern

Spanner bar (rotator)

Trampoline

Daggerboard

Toe loop

Tiller connecting bar

Hound fitting

Diamond wires

Spreaders

Shrouds

Mast ball

F16 with parts labelled

Assuming your catamaran has been delivered as two hulls, a mast and a box of equipment, this chapter gives you a general overview of what to do, whether it be a single-handed or a two-person cat. Specific rigging manuals are available from the manufacturer to help you.

STANDARD CAT

ASSEMBLING THE PLATFORM

To put the cat together you need to:
- Attach the beams to the hulls
- Attach the trampoline to the platform

The exact method of attaching the beams to the hulls and the trampoline may differ slightly by type of catamaran, but a common way is shown in the photo sequence.

Once the cat has been put together, it is a good idea to familiarise yourself with the various positions and adjustments available on your catamaran: the mainsheet and jibsheet jamming blocks, the toestrap positions and, most important of all, the method of raising and lowering the rudders (and boards, if fitted).

Assembling The Dart Platform

1 Lay out the various parts and identify them

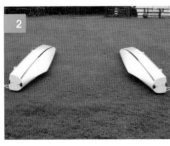

2 Position the hulls side-by-side about 3 metres apart on level ground

3 Prepare to insert the main beam by taking the pressure off the retaining clip

4 Insert the main beam into one hull with the mast ball facing up. (In some cases the beams are a frame or are bolted directly to the hulls)

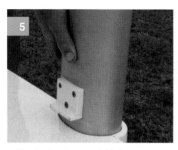

5 Push the beam right home to the thrust pad

6 Insert the rear beam with the traveller facing up

7 Move the remaining hull into position and slide it into the free end of the beams, keeping the hull in line during the process

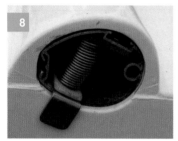

8 Make sure the retaining clip is located correctly

9 Put on the rubber sealing rings and hatch covers

10 Feed the trampoline into the track on the main beam

11 Slide the trampoline into the tracks on the hulls

12 Insert the trampoline tube

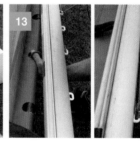

13 Lace the trampoline tube to the rear beam... running the lacing through fittings as shown

14 Tension the trampoline lacing: remember the trampoline will stretch during use and will need re-tensioning at a later date

15 Add the toe straps by drawing the line through the hole and back through the loop in the strap

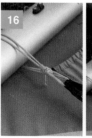

16 Draw the free end of the line through the loop in the other end and tie it securely... and insert the paddle in the storage bag

Alternative Systems

Other classes have different ways of assembling the platform. Where bolts are used, line the holes up carefully making sure the threads are greased and not cross threaded.

On the Hobie the platform support cup is placed in the beam upright, tapped into place and then bolted

On some other cats, the beam is bolted to the hull

Use a torque wrench to tighten the bolts to the stated specification

There are also different ways of attaching the trampoline, but with all it is vital to re-tension it regularly.

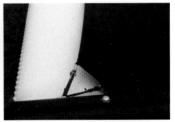

The Hobie 15 has lacing down the centre of the trampoline

The Nacra 17 has lacing to attach the trampoline to the hulls

The Topaz trampoline is tightened at the corners

ATTACHING & RAISING THE MAST

To attach the mast you need to:

- Attach the halyards (if required)
- Attach the mast to the mast ball
- Attach the standing rigging
- Raise the mast and secure the standard rigging

Once again, some of this may differ from cat to cat, but the basic approach is shown in the photo sequence.

1 If necessary, feed the halyards up the mast

2 And through the appropriate sheaves

3 Lay the heel of the mast onto the mast ball with the mast laying aft; support the mast tip on a trestle or similar; take care not to rest the mast on the rear beam without substantial padding

4 Place the mast foot onto the ball and secure it (usually with a retaining pin): this prevents the heel jumping off the ball when it is being raised

5 Attach the hound fitting / standing rigging, checking all hound shackles and rigging links are secure and in good condition

6 Take the shrouds to the hull shroud plates, making sure there are no kinks or twists in the wires

7 Connect the shrouds to the shroud plates on the hulls

8 Lay the trapeze wires over the main beam along with the forestay

9 Feed the jib halyard through the locking ring on the forestay

10 Secure the bridle wires to the bow plates so it is ready for use

11 Raise the mast with one person guiding the mast forward from the stern and another person pulling the mast upright from the bow using the trapeze handles or forestay

12 When the mast is upright connect the forestay to the bridle wires with a shackle or lanyard

13 When all is secure, remove the retaining mast heel pin

14 Clip the trapeze ring to the shockcord

15 Rig the restraining line

ATTACHING THE SHEETS & CONTROL LINES

 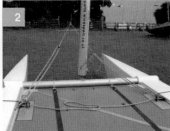 

1 Attach the jib blocks *2 And thread the jib sheets* *3 Tie one end of the traveller line to the mast foot*

4 Run the traveller line under the trampoline *5 And through the traveller* *6 Attach the mainsheet to the traveller*

 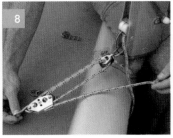 

7 Tie the end of the mainsheet to the traveller line using a sheet bend *8 Attach the downhaul to the foot of the mast* *9 Tie on the righting line to the foot of the mast*

ATTACHING THE RUDDERS & TILLERS

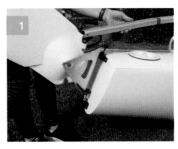 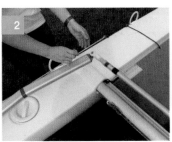 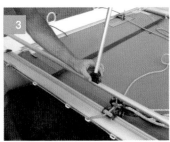

1 Attach the rudders making sure the retaining clips are operating *2 Secure the connecting bar to the tiller arms* *3 Attach the tiller extension to the connecting bar*

HOISTING THE SAILS

Most catamarans can be moved on a simple trolley placed under the hulls at the balance point. The bows then serve as a 'handle' allowing the team to manoeuvre around the boar park efficiently. Before hoisting the sails move your cat closer to the water with the bows pointing into the wind. Protect the keel of each hull and slide the trolley forward to ensure the catamaran sits securely, ready for hoisting the sails.

Balance the hulls on the trolley and use the bows as a 'handle'

Raising The Mainsail

To raise the mainsail:

- Insert the battens (cats generally have tapered battens, so the thinnest part goes in first).
- Hoist the sail with the halyard and secure it.
- Connect the spanner line, downhaul system, boom (if you have one) and any other sail control, but NOT the mainsheet.

The detail of this is shown in the photo sequence.

Most catamarans have some form of halyard locking system at the head of the sail to reduce halyard stretch, but the exact mechanism may vary from class to class.

Raising The Mainsail On A Dart

1 Feed the battens into the mainsail and tie off

2 Push the loose ends into the batten pockets

3 Test the tension by 'popping' the battens – they should just flick from one side to the other; if they don't: tighten or loosen them as appropriate

4 Shackle the main halyard to the head of the mainsail; if you have a knot as shown, make sure the knot is facing aft so that the lock at the top of the mast engages the ring

5 Feed the luff of the mainsail into the upper mast luff groove opening

6 Raise the mainsail, feeding the sail luff into the mast groove as you go: more effort will be needed as the sail feeds further up the mast due to friction and the sail shape

7 When fully hoisted, the ring will slip over the lock hook at the masthead

8 Feed the bottom of the mainsail luff into the lower luff groove on the mast

9 Attach the downhaul system to the sail tack, but do not tighten it at this stage: tensioning the luff creates a wing shape in the sail and creates power encouraging the cat to try to sail on land!

10 Attach the spanner line to the mast spanner bar fitting

Alternative Systems

Other classes have different halyard locking systems.

The halyard locking system on the Hobie

Raising The Jib

If you have a jib, to raise it:

- Attach the jib halyard and identify any lock or adjustment system.
- Raise the jib and connect any locking system.
- Tension the jib using the downhaul.
- Connect the jib sheets.

The detail of this is shown in the photo sequence.

If there is a locking or adjustment system, this may vary from class to class.

1 Attach the jib halyard to the head of the sail: if there is a hook, the opening should face aft

2 Raise the jib, attaching the hanks (if fitted) or, in some cases closing the zip system as you go

3 Continue to raise the jib

4 If you have a locking system, with the jib raised, pull the clew and release the halyard to drop the hook onto the ring

5 Secure the tack of the jib with the jib downhaul, adjusting the tension to suit the wind (see p104)

6 Attach the jibsheet to the clew of the jib

HIGH PERFORMANCE CAT

Putting a performance cat together follows exactly the same principles that we have covered in the previous section. The controls may be more sophisticated, but the principles are the same.

The jib will probably have a zip rather than hanks

There may be a clewboard for different jib sheeting angles

And a track for the jibsheets to attach to

There will be a boom and the mainsheet system will be more complicated with more purchases

Instead of a spanner line there will usually be a spanner bar for great sensitivity in adjustment

But the greatest difference will be the addition of a gennaker.

GENNAKERS / ASYMMETRIC SPINNAKERS

Your cat may have been specifically designed to carry a gennaker, or you may have a 'bolt-on' accessory kit. Either way, you need to set up the additional equipment and rig it correctly for smooth running and maximum performance.

The techniques and systems used on gennaker cats has seen significant steps forward in development along with the way gennakers are used to create added performance. The following information provides a broad outline on what to expect, best practise, and is best adopted in conjunction with specific information from the manufacturer.

The gennaker is primarily for downwind sailing,

and is designed to produce power and lift. The material is light, has minimum water absorption properties and low stretch characteristics.

The shape and cut of a gennaker may vary depending on the downwind sailing angles it is designed to perform in. The front edge (the luff) is designed to curl (collapse) one third of the way down its length; simply ease the sheet until the luff starts to curl to achieve the best performance.

If the sail is cut flat you can sail closer to the wind but it is more sensitive to the luff collapsing, making it harder to set. Gennakers are under constant development, improving power input and efficiency.

Catamaran Preparation

The gennaker is a light weight sail that is hoisted and recovered many times while on the water. To protect the sail from snagging and being damaged, identify and address any areas of the platform or rig that could cause sail damage:

- Tape up anything that might snag the gennaker: safety rings, shackles, shroud adjusters, hound fixings etc.
- Shorten the mainsail battens to the minimum (to minimise the risk of the gennaker getting caught on them) and round any free edges.
- Use silicon spay on any surfaces the gennaker will pass over, like the gennaker recover hoop and stock.
- Use elastic 'ties' to prevent the sail or halyard hooking round the hounds, diamond spreaders, the lower diamond tensioners, or any other projections.

 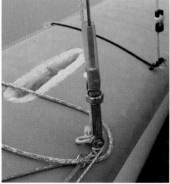 

Tape all sharp edges and anything that might snag the gennaker   *Have tubing over the shrouds*   *Use clearance elastic at the diamonds and shrouds*

In the initial stages add some downwind tell tales to the gennaker pole bridle wires to help you 'see' changes in apparent wind. Site them carefully so that they do not foul the sheets or the sail itself.

Attaching The Gennaker

1 Attach the gennaker's head to the halyard with a bowline or a stopper ball to prevent the head being drawn into the halyard block near the top of the mast   *2 Secure the tack to the outhaul line coming from the end of the pole, using a bowline or stopper ball to prevent the tack being pulled into the pole / block*   *3 If you are using a chute recovery system, attach the recovery line from the chute via the recovery patches on the sail, checking it runs under the gennaker sheets*

If there is a luff line fitted, stretch the gennaker's luff loosely between two people and adjust the luff line to be marginally tighter than the luff tape. This prevents the tape stretching.

Choose sheets for the gennaker that are non-absorbent, thick enough to handle in a range of conditions, and a different colour from the other lines on the trampoline.

There are various methods of attaching the gennaker sheets to the clew. The most basic is a bowline or similar using both ends of the gennaker sheet through the clew eye. Alternatively snagging can be minimised and weight reduced by sewing a short tail line midway to the gennaker sheet, or creating a soft loop from the core of the rope, and then threading this loop through the clew eye and the gennaker sheets back through.

Choose the position of the gennaker sheet turning blocks (if available) to provide a sheeting angle that controls the foot and the leech.

The best way to observe this is to view the sail reaction ashore, looking at the way it opens and closes during adjustment.

To alter the sheeting angle you can either move the turning block or use a barber hauler line.

Barber haulers are a means of on-the-water adjustment to sheeting angles, offering limited control of leech twist and sail slot. By careful adjustment, fine tuning of the gennaker sheeting angles can be made relevant to the position of the gennaker and the wind conditions.

The optimum way of attaching the gennaker sheets

Thread the gennaker sheets through the pulleys

Hoisting Systems

There are two main systems of hoisting the gennaker: two-line and one-line.

Two-line system: Here you have a separate halyard and a separate gennaker tackline. In essence you can hoist the sail up and out independently providing flexibility as to the fastest and safest way to hoist and drop. For speed the most efficient way is normally tack out first on the hoist and halyard drop first on the drop.

The disadvantage is that the two-line system is slightly slower to operate and less automatic for the team.

One-line system: The one line system hoists the gennaker up and also out to the end of the pole at the same time. The advantage is that there is only one line to pull and simplicity. However, using the one-line system reduces flexibility of adjustment and independent control of the tack line and halyard.

Tidy lines on the platform area are less likely to foul during hoists and drops, so a block and shockcord takeaway system provides a simple solution.

Checking The Hoist

Prevention is better than cure so, whenever possible, carry out a dry land hoist to confirm that everything is correct: all halyards and lines are on the outside and running smoothly.

Next, check the sail's luff tension when fully hoisted. A good starting guide is to hold the luff edge in your hand and then just be able to rotate your hand through 90°, wrapping the sail around your knuckles. Too much luff tension will destroy the sail shape, too little and you will have difficulty in setting the gennaker correctly.

Once you have the correct tension, it is a good idea to mark the halyard when hoisted so that you can easily hoist it with the right luff tension. However, the luff length depends on the distance from the end of the gennaker pole to the halyard block near the top of the mast so, if you change the mast rake or pole height, this will affect the distance between the two points and you will need to reset the halyard mark.

Storing The Gennaker

There are two methods: a bag or a chute:

- A bag is simple and often used on longer distance races or very large gennakers. It does require good boat handling.
- A chute removes a lot of the recovery work, keeps the platform area clear and is excellent for short course racing. The small trade-off is that it adds weight and windage in front of the mast.

The chute is normally rigged on the port side, giving a windward drop and leeward hoist on port-hand courses. The recovery line system tends to bunch the gennaker as it enters the chute increasing friction. A good chute system will reduce this friction as much as possible. Spraying silicon around the chute mouth and sock as the gennaker is recovered into the chute on the beach will help.

If you are using a bag system, stow the gennaker neatly, preferably on the leeward side for your first hoist.

Tidy and secure the gennaker sheets to prevent them being washed overboard.

Hoist the gennaker ashore to check all the lines are led correctly

Use the 'hand twist' method to assess the luff tension

Pole Tension

Depending on the length and size of the pole, a series of bridle wires are used to support its length. The wires attached to the outboard end control the height and restrain the sideways movement. Mid-pole bridle wires help prevent the middle of the pole flexing under gennaker load. For light and thin poles, pre-bend is advisable to stiffen the pole. Try not to use the pole end as a trolley handle when launching!

Pre-bend in the pole helps keep it straight when the gennaker comes under load

Take a careful look at the photograph on this page. You will see that:

- The helmsman sits on the windward side of the cat (to balance the wind pushing on the sail).
- The helmsman always holds the tiller in his aft (back) hand in a 'dagger' grip. He steers with the tiller.
- The helmsman holds the mainsheet in his forward (front) hand. The mainsheet adjusts the angle of the sail to the centreline of the catamaran.
- The crew uses their weight to prevent the cat heeling. This means sitting to windward in strong winds, to leeward in light winds.
- The crew holds the jibsheet. The jibsheet controls the angle of the jib to the centreline of the catamaran.
- The jib and mainsail are roughly parallel.

If you are sailing a single-handed cat, the theory is no different, it's just that there's only one of you and you might not have a jib.

HOW DOES A CATAMARAN SAIL?

A sailing craft is rather like a car: it requires fuel and an engine. In the case of a catamaran the fuel is the wind and the engine is the sails. The stronger the wind the more power is produced from the sails and the faster the cat will go ... providing you do not lose control and capsize!

The forward motion is produced by the flow of moving air over the sails, from front to back. Air flowing over the windward side of each sail causes pressure whilst air flowing over the leeward side causes suction. The resulting force is in the direction of arrows A and B in the diagram and is at right angles to each sail.

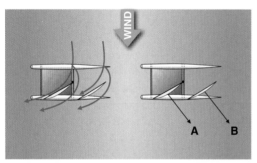

Wind abeam: wind flowing over the sails & direction of force

This force pushes the cat forward and sideways. The forward motion propels the catamaran towards its goal and the sideways force is resisted by the water pressure on the shaped hull or underwater foils.

The weight of the helmsman and crew on the windward side counteracts the heeling (capsize)

effect. The stronger the wind the more the catamaran wants to heel over and the further out the crew must lean. Eventually a point is reached where, to produce more power, the crew must trapeze on the side of the hull.

Alternatively, the helmsman can ease the sail and spill some wind, but this will reduce the power and normally make the cat slow down.

When sailing against the wind, the sails are pulled right in and the forces A and B are at near right-angles to the cat. The sideways force is now at its strongest, so you need full extension of the boards or make maximum use of the underwater hull shape (i.e. skegs) to stop the catamaran going sideways.

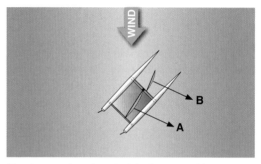

Beating against the wind & direction of force

When sailing with the wind coming from behind, the sails are eased out and the force is now pushing directly the way the catamaran wants to move, so no significant use of the boards is needed and the skegs have no function other than directional stability.

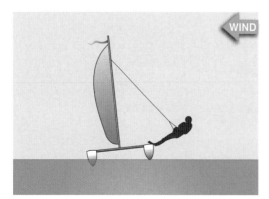

Crew on the trapeze

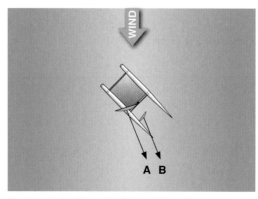

Running with the wind & direction of force

HOW CAN I STEER?

When a cat is sailing straight, the water flows past the rudders undisturbed. When the rudders are turned, the water is deflected. The water hitting the rudders pushes them, and the back of the cat, in direction C. The bows turn to the right.

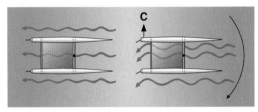

Rudders straight & rudders turned

In short, pulling the tiller extension towards you turns the bows away from you, and vice versa. Note that the rudders can work only when the cat is moving and water is flowing past them.

HOW CAN I STOP?

It is the wind flowing over the sails that makes the catamaran go forward. To stop the cat, take the flow away from the sails either by letting out the sheets (first option) or by altering course gently towards the wind (second option). In a catamaran it is best to slow down but not quite stop since, if you stop, you will be unable to steer.

HOW CAN I TELL WHICH WAY THE WIND IS BLOWING?

Everything in sailing is related to the wind direction. You can tell which way the wind is blowing by various means: the feel of it on your face, the wave direction or using a burgee (flag). Remember, the burgee points towards the wind (i.e. pointing to the direction it is coming from).

As you start sailing and pick up speed, your forward momentum has the effect of 'creating' wind just as, if you stuck your hand out of a moving car, you would feel 'wind' on your hand, even if the real wind was blowing across you path. The real wind and the wind created by your forward motion combine to create 'apparent wind' from a direction somewhere between the two. This is particularly relevant to reaching and sailing downwind and we will come back to it later.

POINTS OF SAILING

Look at the diagram on the following page. There are three basic points of sailing:
- **Reaching** – the cat sails across wind.
- **Beating** – the cat sails as close as it can towards the wind.
- **Running** – the cat sails with the wind behind it.

REACHING

When reaching, the catamaran sails at right angles to the wind, which is blowing from behind your back if you are sitting on the windward side. The sails should be about halfway out and the boards, if fitted, should be about halfway up.

BEATING

If you change course towards the wind, you must push the tiller extension away from you, put the boards down (if fitted) and pull in the sails as you make the turn from a reach. You can go on turning towards the wind until the sails are pulled right in, but not flapping. You are now as close to the wind as you can sail: beating.

If you try to turn further towards the wind you enter a 'no-go zone'. The sails flap and your cat stops.

If you want to reach a point that is upwind of your current position you have to beat in a zigzag fashion, as shown in the diagram.

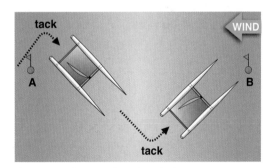

Catamaran beating into the wind

At the end of each 'zig' your catamaran turns through an angle of 90°. This is called a tack. The cat turns 'through' the wind – the sails move across to the other side of the cat and the team must move their weight across the cat for balance.

RUNNING / DOWNWIND

From a reach, you may wish to change course away from the wind. Raise the boards 75% (if fitted) and let the sails out as you turn. You can go on turning until the wind is coming from behind your catamaran. Then you are running.

If you turn further, your catamaran will eventually gybe. The wind blows from the other side of the cat, the sail will cross over and you must move your weight across to balance the hull and the sail pressure.

Reaching

Beating

Running

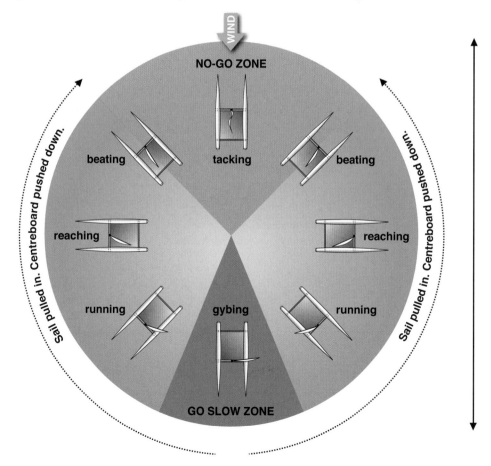

Try to choose a day with a gentle breeze for your first sail. Force 4 or above would be unsuitable. Here we have shown the speed in miles per hour (mph), but strength of breeze can be measured in various formats.

Beaufort No.	General description	On land	At sea	Speed (mph)
0	Calm	Calm; smoke rises vertically	Sea like a mirror	<1
1	Light air	Direction of wind shown by smoke drift but not wind vanes	Ripples	1-3
2	Light breeze	Wind felt on face; leaves rustle	Small wavelets	4-7
3	Gentle breeze	Leaves and small twigs in constant motion; wind extends light flags	Large wavelets; crests begin to break	8-12
4	Moderate	Raises dust and loose paper; small branches are moved	Small waves, becoming longer, fairly requent white horses	13-18
5	Fresh breeze	Small trees in leaf begin to sway	Moderate waves, many white horses, chance of some spray	19-24
6	Strong breeze	Large branches in motion; umbrellas used with difficulty	Large waves begin to form; the white foam crests are more extensive everywhere; probably some spray	25-31
7	Near gale	Whole trees in motion	Sea heaps up and white foam from breaking waves begins to be blown in streaks	32-38

A reservoir or estuary is a good place to learn to sail. If there's a sailing school that specialises in catamaran beginners' courses, that's even better. If you are learning on the open sea try to avoid an offshore wind (wind blowing from shore to sea) – you may get blown a long way from the shore.

PERSONAL CLOTHING

Typically you wear same protective clothing for cat sailing as you would for other small boat sailing disciplines including (and essentially) a buoyancy aid, whatever the conditions.

You might need a wetsuit, spray top, rash vest, sailing boots and gloves and a hat depending on where you sail and the conditions. Even if the conditions look perfect it is best to take some protective clothing with you as conditions can change.

If you are the type who feels the cold, add extra thermal layers under your spraysuit or consider a drysuit with thermal suit underneath. Better be warm and comfortable than cold and miserable!

As your confidence and ability increase you will need a trapeze harness. Trapeze harnesses come in all shapes and sizes: one size does not fit all. Try before you buy considering back support, spreader bar option and a quick release hook safety feature.

A buoyancy aid is essential; a wetsuit is also a good idea

OFF YOU GO

Rig your catamaran as described on p26-28 and launch as described on p52-55.

As soon as you can, start sailing on a reach, with the wind blowing at right angles to the cat. Choose a goal, sheet in the mainsail until the telltales at the top of the sail are streaming (see p43), likewise the jib (if you have one), and go!

Practise adjusting the sails and steering. Try to get the 'feel' for your catamaran, particularly using your weight to balance the wind in the sails.

Catamarans can go quite fast so it is important that you keep an eye out to see where you are in relation to your launch point and other water users. Eyes out of the boat are better than eyes looking in the boat, so make sure that you do not get too involved in looking at the sails and rig, sorting the ropes, etc and loosing focus on where you are heading and what is around you – with embarrassing and potentially expensive consequences.

If you are sailing single handed, most of the same things apply as they do when sailing with a crew, but you only have one pair of hands to do all the jobs normally shared between helm and crew. So sailing single handed is as much about planning and organisation as it is about technique. You may only have one sail (or two if you carry a gennaker), but launch and recovery in particular are harder. Throughout the book we will offer advice for single handers when it is different to sailing two up.

Single-handed sailing on a calm day

SAILING POSITION

Whilst we all develop our own individual techniques it is a good idea to begin from a proven starting point. This is especially true of cat sailing where good technique will allow you to focus on other areas such as boatspeed, manoeuvring and race tactics in the future.

As **helm**, steer with the tiller extension on your shoulder, your back hand holding it in a dagger grip. Your front hand is for constant adjustment of the mainsheet. This allows you to lean out, adjust your mainsheet, and make controlled alterations of the traveller line. It is also a good idea to keep all excess control lines close to your body to stop them being washed overboard.

As **crew**, hold the jibsheet in your back hand (unless trapezing off the stern quarter of the catamaran). Your front hand is used for adjusting the trapeze height (if using a trapeze).

The positions of helm and crew on the platform will change depending on the wind strength and sailing direction.

MEDIUM WINDS

- The helmsman sits on the deck of the windward hull with their feet under the toestraps.
- The tiller extension is held in their back hand in a dagger grip, while the mainsheet is controlled by the forward hand.
- The crew is also positioned on the windward side but has their backside over the edge of

the gunwale with their feet under the toestraps and the jibsheet held in their back hand.

LIGHT WINDS

Should the wind become lighter the crew will need to move their weight towards the centreline of your catamaran, and if necessary to leeward, to keep the cat level and balanced.

Light-wind position, further forward and crew to leeward

STRONG WINDS

- The helmsman moves their backside over the gunwale to sit out further and to help keep a stable position on the cat.
- The crew gives extra leverage by using the trapeze wire with their feet on the gunwale. To do this they need to wear a trapeze harness to which the trapeze wire is connected.

Medium-wind position, with both helm and crew on the windward hull

Strong-wind position, with the crew on the wire and the helm hiked out

YOUR FIRST TACK

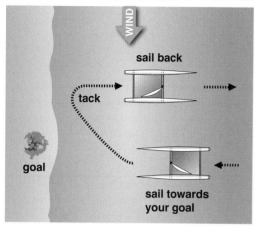

Tacking

As you approach your goal you will need to turn your cat round. You can do this by turning to the right or to the left, into the wind or away from the wind.

The most controlled turn is into the wind, so turn the front of the cat through the wind and, once the turn is completed, head back to where you have sailed: this turn is called a tack.

Steer the cat into position ready for tacking by sailing as close to the wind as possible but with boatspeed. To do this: pull the sails in firmly as you steer your catamaran towards the wind and identify the edge of the 'no-go zone'. If you reach a point where the jib is about to collapse at the front (the luff), you will know that your cat is entering the 'no-go zone' as it will begin to slow down. Sail on the edge of the 'no-go zone' to maintain your speed.

Check that the area around you is clear and initiate the tacking manoeuvre by pushing the tiller away from you firmly to about 45° and hold it there until your cat has passed through the 'no-go zone' and is ready to sail on the new tack, with the wind

1 Get the cat sailing close to the wind, with boatspeed

2 Steer the cat through the wind

3 Change sides and transfer the tiller extension into your other hand

4 Sail off on the other tack

on the other side of the sails. During the turning process both crew and helm should move across the trampoline to the new windward side of the catamaran. The crew releases the jibsheet from the original side, crossing it to the same side as the mainsail once the mainsail battens are seen to 'pop' and take up their new airflow shape. Tacking is described in more detail on p65-69.

Now head back to your original starting point. To get your catamaran sailing across the wind again, pull the tiller extension towards you and ease the sails out until the jib is just about to flap and the telltales on either side of the mainsail (at the top) are flowing horizontally.

If the cat for any reason does not complete the tack – that is, does not turn through the 'no-go zone' – you may have to re-start by getting the cat sailing fast again on the original course before you make a second attempt.

If you feel your cat is going too fast or you start to lose control, ease out the mainsheet and the jibsheet to slow down, but keep the cat heading across the wind towards your goal. When you get close to your starting point repeat the procedure of tacking through the 'no-go zone', and sail back out to your original goal. Remember that, before tacking, you must first sail your cat as close to the wind as possible. Make sure that you are well clear of other craft and the shore during this exercise.

GETTING OUT OF 'IRONS'

There are various reasons why a beginner may not complete a successful tack and these are listed on p69.

One major fault is not having the sails in tight as the cat turns into the tack, so the catamaran does not even reach head to wind. The symptom of this is the bow being blown back on to its original course. In this case, pull the sails firmly in, get up speed and try again.

If, however, the cat reaches head to wind but there is insufficient boatspeed to complete the tack, the cat will become stuck head to wind ('in irons') and start to drift backwards. If this happens:

- Maintain the jib in on the original side to help force the bow round.
- Ease the mainsheet.
- As the cat drifts backwards, reverse the rudders to turn your cat onto its new heading.
- Having achieved a three-point turn, straighten the rudders, release the jib and cross it over to the same side as the mainsail, pull in both sails and head off in the direction of your goal.

See photo sequence, below.

1 Initiate tack by pushing rudders

2 When cat starts going backwards reverse the rudders and change sides

3 When on the new tack straighten rudders, sheet in and sail away

GYBING

Once you have mastered the art of tacking, try doing the opposite manoeuvre: gybing. Reach across the wind towards your goal but this time, instead of turning the cat towards the wind, turn it away from the wind. The turn is called a gybe.

Turn your cat from the beam reach by pulling the tiller extension towards you and at the same time, easing out the sails and the traveller. Watch the bridle wire wind indicator and keep turning until the indicator is 90° across the catamaran – you are now sailing downwind 'cat-style'. Some would call this broad reaching.

If the cat is turned further downwind the sails will stall and the cat will slow down considerably, making it harder to gybe. The downwind indicator will display this by blowing further forward than 90° across the catamaran.

As you prepare to gybe, first make sure that you have sufficient room for the manoeuvre and that there are no other boats in the way. Have the sails as far out as possible. Pull the tiller extension towards you and move immediately across the cat. Let the

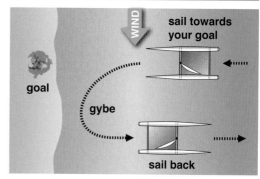

Gybing

sails cross the catamaran, then centralise the rudders. Gybing is described in more detail on p78-81.

Once you have completed your gybe do not forget to check where you are heading, then set the mainsail and jib so that the telltales are flowing on the sails.

In force 2 to 3 you may consider gybing an easier option to tacking but it is important that you can do both with ease and fluency, in all conditions – so practise.

1 Turn away from the wind and begin to move across the cat

2 Change hands on the tiller extension and hold the mainsheet falls

3 While still turning, control the mainsheet falls

4 Sail off on the other gybe

INTRODUCTION TO C.A.T.

KEY ASPECTS

A good way of remembering what you need to think about when sailing a catamaran is **C.A.T.**

C Crew weight – position around the catamaran, fore and aft, inboard and outboard.
A Airflow – the position of the sails to give optimum performance.
T Technique – how best to sail the cat given the sea, wind, tides and movements of other craft.

C.A.T. is relevant to all points of sailing and worth remembering when you are on the water. Whether you are a novice cat sailor or racing guru, when you get C.A.T. right you will be sailing fast!

CREW WEIGHT

Look to keep the hulls 'tuned' correctly fore-and-aft by moving your weight to keep the hulls parallel to the water. Lean in or out and trim the sheets to keep the windward hull just kissing the water. Good hull and sail trim will give the catamaran a good turn of speed and make it easy to control.

Try to keep the windward hull kissing the water

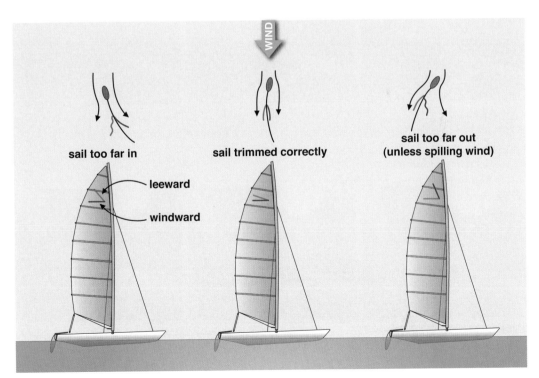

WIND

sail too far in   sail trimmed correctly   sail too far out (unless spilling wind)

leeward

windward

Airflow as shown by telltales

AIRFLOW

When setting the sails, pull them in to prevent the sails flapping, then 'fine tune' using the telltales. Telltales, sometimes called woollies or sail streamers, are simply threads of wool or thin strips of spinnaker sailcloth, attached to the sails to show clearly the effect of the air passing over them. Their job is to help the helm or crew read the airflow over the sails more clearly.

The telltales on both sides of each sail should constantly stream backwards, demonstrating a smooth passage of air over both surfaces.

- If the leeward telltale starts to fall or circle, the air flowing over this side of the sail is disturbed and the sail should be eased out.
- If the windward telltale stalls the sail should be pulled in to smooth the airflow.

In the case of the mainsail, you should start by adjusting the mainsheet to make the top set of telltales react correctly. As you improve you will be able to make the majority of lower telltales flow correctly too by using the mainsheet, downhaul, batten tension and traveller position.

The jib can also be sheeted for maximum efficiency using its own telltales as a guide: again, they should be streaming both sides.

TECHNIQUE

This covers everything else, from where you steer, where you position the centreboards and so on.

Controlling The Tiller & Mainsheet

It is a good idea to practise controlling the tiller and mainsheet on land and get into the right habits.

In Light & Medium Winds

1 Normally hold the tiller extension over your shoulder with your aft hand and control the mainsheet with your fore hand

2 To sheet in, haul in the mainsheet with your forward hand

3 Clamp it against the tiller extension with your thumb

4 Then catch hold of the mainsheet below the point where you have clamped it

5 And haul away again

6 Until you are again in your normal sailing position with the tiller extension in your aft hand and mainsheet in your fore hand

In Stronger Winds

In heavier winds, you may need to use both hands to haul in the sheet.

1 Brace the tiller extension against your shoulder and use your aft hand on the mainsheet as well

2 Haul in the mainsheet with both hands

3 Clamp the sheet with your tiller hand

4 And then grab the mainsheet lower down with your mainsheet hand

Adjusting The Traveller

1 To control the traveller, use your tiller hand to clamp the mainsheet while you pick up the traveller line

2 Uncleat the traveller

3 Let out the traveller to suit the sailing conditions and then cleat it again

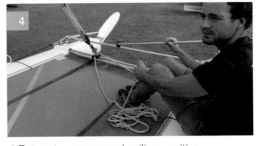

4 Return to your normal sailing position

SAILING A SQUARE COURSE

When you feel happy reaching, tacking and gybing you are ready to try other points of sailing. One good way to practise is to sail round a square 'course'.

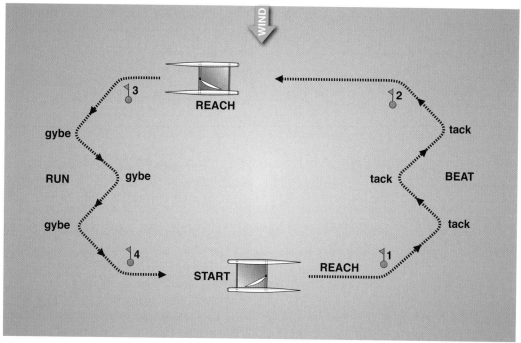

Sailing a square course

THE REACH

We start off on a reach with the traveller centred. (At a later stage we can use the traveller more efficiently to improve the catamaran's performance.) Sail across the wind towards your goal.

Crew weight: The cat needs to be balanced equally on each hull with the fore-and-aft trim adjusted, so that the catamaran is level in the water. It is a good tip to look at the transom to see if it is dragging. If the breeze increases the cat will accelerate, causing the bows to dip, so be prepared to move your weight aft to compensate for the downward pressure on the bows.

Airflow: Adjust the sheeting of the mainsail and jib so that the telltales are streaming both sides.

Technique: Plan to keep looking ahead, and allow for any current, sideways drift or waves. If the windward hull starts to lift from the water, move your body weight outboard and, if necessary, ease the mainsail to control the heeling moment. If you have boards position them half way.

Sailing on a reach with the hulls balanced and the sails sheeted correctly

THE BEAT

When you reach your goal you will need to sail against the wind by beating, that is, zig-zagging your way to a new goal further upwind by tacking.

Turn the hulls towards the wind by pushing the tiller away from you and sheet in the sails to correct the airflow. This will direct your cat towards the 'no-go zone' and allow you to start your progress to windward.

Crew weight: Keep the catamaran balanced by moving your crew weight inboard and outboard as required. (The sideways force on the cat can be increased and the crew may need to go out on the trapeze to stop it heeling over.) Trim the cat by positioning your combined crew weight so that the catamaran is level: normally you will have to be further forward than when reaching.

Airflow: With the sails pulled in firmly, point your catamaran towards the wind until the windward telltale on the jib begins to stall. At this point back off a few degrees to keep the cat sailing as close to the wind as possible, on the edge of the 'no-go zone'.

Technique: To sail efficiently against the wind concentrate on sailing the fine line between entering the 'no-go zone' and pointing too far away from the wind. You will have to make the decision when to tack and sail on the other side of the 'no-go zone' to reach your goal – normally this new course is at about 90° to your previous heading.

If you have boards lower them fully to reduce sideways forces.

When you get to your windward goal you can relax and go back to a reach, as covered earlier. Don't forget to pull your boards (if fitted) to the mid position and use C.A.T. to get the most from your craft.

DOWNWIND

Your next goal, downwind of your current position, will complete your square course but you need to sail efficiently.

Catamarans can sail with the wind coming from directly behind, but it is usually faster to zig-zag downwind using the speed generated to your advantage. For more detail see p70-74.

Crew weight: Make sure that the cat is balanced evenly and move aft so the transoms are only just out of the water.

Airflow: Position the traveller right out to reduce sail twist. Ease the mainsail until it is just touching the shrouds and ease the jibsheet as much as possible without the jib telltales stalling.

You may find it easier with the crew on the leeward side of the catamaran depending on wind conditions.

Technique: You could decide to sail straight downwind to begin with, but you will soon learn that it is quicker to zig-zag, keeping the sails at 90° to the apparent wind. To achieve that, focus on keeping the downwind indicator between the bridle wires at approximately 90° to the cat. When you gybe you will head off at near 90° to your previous course. If you have boards raise them about 50–75%.

Beating with the cat level, sails tight in, sailing on the edge of the 'no go zone'

Downwind, sail with the sails approximately 90° to the apparent wind

HEAVING-TO

'Heaving-to' is a sensible option if you:
- Need a rest!
- Need to stop to adjust something.
- Find yourself in a position where sailing could be dangerous.

The effect is to depower the sails and set them to balance each other so that the catamaran simply drifts slowly sideways downwind. To do this on a catamaran:
- Ease the mainsheet and traveller line.
- Pull the jib to the wrong side of the cat (the windward side) using the windward jibsheet.
- Position the rudders so that they try to turn the catamaran into the wind and hold them there (i.e. push them away from you).

Now the sails will balance each other and, if the cat tries to move forward, the rudders will steer it up towards the wind, which will kill the speed.

Try heaving-to in an area away from any obstacles or lee shores – it is very relaxing after zooming around! You can also depower the mainsail by releasing the downhaul line.

'Heaving-to' allows you to rest or adjust equipment

When single handed without a jib carry out the same procedure using the mainsheet only.

RETURNING TO THE SHORE

You have had a good sail and are now on your way back to the beach. Choose a cross-wind landing so the catamaran arrives on a reach in an area clear of obstacles and other craft. Landing is described on p97-100.

There are many different cats ideal for your first sail

Most modern catamarans are made of reinforced fibreglass (G.R.P.) or similar, so there is no time-consuming varnishing or painting required. However, a catamaran is a fast, hi-tech machine that requires regular inspection and general care, as would a fast car.

On a daily basis, check:
- The hulls are empty of water, and the bungs (if fitted) are screwed in.
- All ring clips are in good condition and taped.
- The trampoline is tight.
- Battens are tensioned before sailing and de-tensioned after the day's sailing.
- The catamaran and fittings are washed down with fresh water.

Every month check:
- The standing rigging shackles / fixings are secure and tight.
- The rudder assembly is in full working order (it kicks up on hitting an underwater obstruction). Check the pintles and gudgeons.
- All jamming cleats and blocks are running freely.
- Any gelcoat damage is repaired.
- Sheets, foot-loops and toestraps are in good condition.
- Wires, rigging and 'eye splices' are not strained, broken or brittle.
- Control lines and systems work smoothly .

Liberal use of WD40, silicon spray or similar, on a monthly basis will make sure you have easy-to-use free-running equipment and make your sailing far more enjoyable.

SAILS

It is advisable to roll the sails when they are not in use, and de-tension the battens for storage. This will prolong the life of most fabrics and maintain the specification of your battens. Rinsing sails and allowing them to dry before storing is recommended, whenever possible.

CATAMARAN STORAGE

If you are storing the catamaran outside, remember the mast and hulls create a huge windage. Tie the cat down with wire or ground screws to prevent it from being blowing over. When not in use for long periods consider lowering the mast and storing it safely.

It is a sensible idea to invest in a quality boat cover to keep the sun off the decks and trampoline, prolonging their life and reducing hull fade.

At the end of the season break your catamaran down into its various parts, repair any gelcoat hull and foil damage before storing the hulls upside down in a sheltered position or supporting them by the hull beam boxes (the strongest part of the catamaran) on a rack at the side of a garage, wall or shed.

The sails should be washed and stored in a dry place ready for next year. Standing and running rigging should be checked for straining around the eye splices, washed, dried and stored.

Tie your cat down securely, either from the shrouds

Or using the trapeze wires, if you have them

TRAILER & CAR TOPPING

Towing rules vary between countries, so check the law. Catamarans up to 2.55 m wide can be towed as a platform in some countries, but check with the trailer manufacturers on the trailer requirements.

Craft wider than this need to be broken down for trailing or tilted at an angle to reduce the over-all width. Spare wheel, storage box and working lighting board are all part of a self-contained trailer package.

Many cats, like the Dart 18, can be towed without being broken down

Alternatively, smaller catamarans can be carried on the roof of the car (subject to car specifications) us-ing a standard roof rack. A two-piece mast will allow you to tow a trailer or caravan behind if you wished or keep the overall length to a minimum.

Smaller cats, like the Sprint 15, can be put on the roof

PART 2
SKILL DEVELOPMENT

With practice you will find you can get afloat quickly and easily in most conditions. How you launch depends on the wind direction relative to the shore. However, a few points will always apply:

- Rig your catamaran on the shore.
- Keep the cat pointing into the wind at all times (and never more than 45° off it).
- Let the sails flap freely and leave the mainsheet unconnected.
- Hulls are very easily damaged: keep them off the ground whenever possible.
- When climbing on board always try to provide some forward motion to aid steering.

LAUNCHING WITH THE WIND
ALONG THE SHORE

This is the easiest wind direction to launch in. Choose a launch area with a cross-shore wind and clear water access.

1 Push the cat into the water on the trolley, keeping the bows within 45 degrees to the wind so that the sails do not fill with wind

2 Remove the trolley and take it back onshore while one of you holds the cat, keeping it clear of the beach

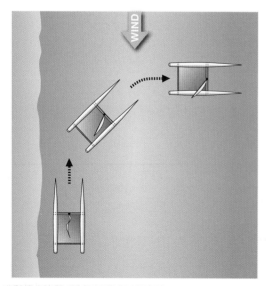

Sailing off with wind along shore

3 With the crew holding the cat head to wind, and the helm on board, tension the mainsail downhaul

4 Check the main and jib sheets are free running and put the boards (if fitted) down slightly

5 Connect the mainsheet system; for your first sail, set the traveller in the centre of the beam

6 Lower the rudders halfway, for limited steering, and place the tiller extension on the side you will be steering from

7 Having checked the area immediately off the beach, the helmsman positions themselves on the windward side of the catamaran holding the tiller extension in their aft hand and the mainsheet in their forward hand

8 The crew pushes the bow across the wind and forward to provide steerage

9 As the boat begins to sail forward the crew climbs on board just behind the shrouds, in front of the helmsman

10 As the sails fill, the helm bears away and you sail away from the beach slowly, using the mainsheet as the accelerator

11 Once into deep water ease the mainsheet and lower the rudders (and boards if fitted) into their sailing positions; until this point your cat is only under partial control and must be sailed slowly

If you are in a single-handed catamaran, then you need to plan your launch even more carefully. Preparation is everything because, once the cat is on the water, you just want to turn off the wind and go. So consider having the mainsheet attached, the daggerboards inserted and raised and the rudders pre-set to the floating position or ready to lower before you launch.

Having a second person to take your trolley once you have launched is a luxury but, if that is not an option and you are unable or unwilling to rest your keel-line on the beach, consider placing an anchor or weight with a buoy or floating anchor line at waist depth which you can hook your catamaran onto while taking your trolley ashore. You can reposition the weight for when you return and the tide has changed if you need to.

1 A single-handed sailor can anchor their cat

2 Leaving their cat anchored when they take the trolley ashore

3 Where it will remain till you return

LAUNCHING WITH AN OFFSHORE WIND

To launch safely with an offshore wind, float your catamaran out backwards with the bows pointing into the wind (towards the shore). All sheets and the traveller should be eased right out and the rudders and boards (if fitted) should be raised.

Position yourselves one on each hull near the bow to raise the stern out of the water; with the bows acting as a sea anchor the cat will drift out backwards to an area of safe water where the team can slide onto the trampoline. Then drop the rudders, turn the catamaran away from the wind and start sailing.

This method is especially useful when you are restricted by other boats or people in the water. Remember, in all but the lightest airs if you try to sail off a windward shore by simply turning your catamaran around and heading downwind, it will probably sail off out of control.

The safest way to launch with an offshore breeze is to 'back out' with the boards and rudders raised

A single-handed sailor can adopt this approach as well.

Remember that, with an offshore wind, the wind will get stronger when you get away from the land.

LAUNCHING WITH AN ONSHORE WIND

This is the most difficult wind direction for launching, because the wind tends to push you back on shore and the direction off the shore is the 'no-go zone'. The crew may need to stand in quite deep water to keep the catamaran afloat with the bows pointing into the wind.

As helmsman, prepare your cat by setting the traveller, preparing the jib and mainsheets and lowering the boards (if fitted) as far as possible. The tack you choose to leave the beach should be the one which allows you to sail most away from the shore. In the diagram, A is better than B because the wind is coming more from the left and A will take you offshore faster.

As crew, holding the windward bow push the bow away from the wind onto the chosen tack. Climb aboard and immediately sheet in the jib, balancing the steering pressure via the mainsheet tension.

Now sail the catamaran slowly to a safe distance offshore before releasing the sheets and lowering the rudders and boards ready for sailing.

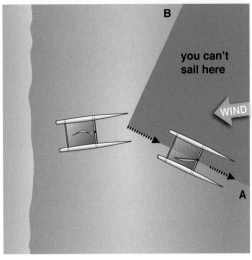

Sailing off with an onshore wind

If single handed, the basic approach is the same, but the helmsman has to do everything and, with only a mainsail, it is vital to maintain airflow over the sail to generate forward power.

1 Hold the boat head to wind   *2 Get the sails filling and climb in*   *3 Sail off slowly*

LAUNCHING WITH AN ONSHORE WIND IN SURF

In some cases you may have to launch from a beach with surf running. This demands a slightly different technique.

Prepare the cat ready to sail with the crew holding the bow. Pick the tack that takes you off the beach most directly and choose a time when the waves are not too big (waves come in sets). When you decide to go, the crew pushes the bow away from the wind and immediately sheet in the main and jib to give maximum balanced power to the sails.

Drive the catamaran off on a close reach, pointing only slightly into the waves as they approach the cat. Boatspeed is paramount: you cannot afford to be turned sideways or the surf will soon capsize you, while if you are pushed backwards you may damage the rudders on the beach. When you are well off, and in sufficient depth, drop your rudders fully; remember that between the waves the water can be quite shallow.

Remember: reaching is sailing across the wind. It is the fastest point of sailing but the jib, mainsail, trim and balance need constant adjustment for maximum speed.

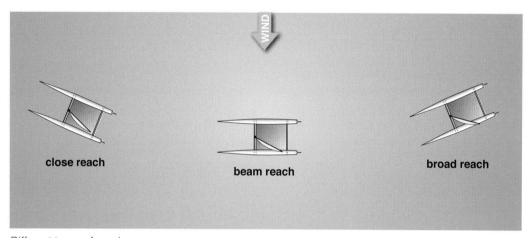

close reach

beam reach

broad reach

Different types of reaches

MEDIUM WINDS

CREW WEIGHT

Constantly move the crew weight fore-and-aft to keep the hulls' waterline level with the water surface – as the wind increases you will need to move slightly aft, but as the wind drops the stern will dig in and you will need to slide forward again. If you are too far forward you will get steering problems, while if you are too far aft you will lose boatspeed.

Most catamarans like to be sailed with the windward hull just clear of the water on a reach, so move your crew weight inboard (and forward) or outboard (and back) to counteract the wind pressure. Try never to heel your catamaran to windward.

AIRFLOW

Set the jib and mainsail so that the telltails on each side of the sails are flowing constantly. Position the main and jib travellers (if fitted) so that, when the sails are pulled in, the top set of telltales are flowing and there is a slight twist in the leech (back edge) of the sails.

The exact position of the traveller will depend on the type of reach (close or broad) and the speed at which the catamaran is travelling but make sure that, when the cat accelerates and the apparent wind moves forward, you can sheet in the sails to reset the telltales without needing to adjust the travellers inboard. Experimenting with the traveller position, sheet tensions and mainsail downhaul will help you create a smooth airflow across the entire surface of the sail.

TECHNIQUE

Concentrate on keeping the sails set to the apparent wind direction, which changes with each alteration in the boatspeed. Try to use your rudders as little as possible, so that they don't act as brakes, and steer round any large waves that might stop your cat. On the race course, steer straight to the next mark (if the other competitors will let you).

Set the boards half up, if you have them. On a close reach push them down a little further and on a broad reach pull them up further if you feel the catamaran is tripping over itself. It is often an option to raise the windward board further. (All these board adjustments apply to any wind strength on a reach.)

Reaching in medium winds: both helm and crew are sitting on the windward hull, the traveller is halfway down and the set of the sails is being controlled with the mainsheet or jib sheet

Reaching in light winds: the helm and crew are well forward and inboard; the sheets need constant adjustment in these conditions

LIGHT WINDS

CREW WEIGHT

The crew will need to sit forward, their head to windward of the mast, and watch the jib constantly. The wind is always changing in speed and direction but at slow speeds the catamaran takes a long time to alter course so, rather than having the helmsman adjusting the tiller all the time, it is often better to adjust the sheets to each wind direction or pressure change first followed by gradual alteration in course.

Generally keep the cat level, but in some instances it may well pay to have the leeward hull slightly deeper in the water to reduce pitching and stabilise the rig.

AIRFLOW

In light winds do not make it too hard for the air to go across the sails. Too much batten tension will make it hard for the air to complete its journey over the sail. The main and jib downhaul tension should be just enough to give sail shape without distorting the sail.

When sailing on a reach in light winds, allow the sails to create as much power as possible: never oversheet (pull the sheets too tight). Oversheeting the mainsail so that the leech is hooked is the most common light wind mistake.

TECHNIQUE

As with medium winds, use as little rudder as possible, though you may want to bear off in a gust. Make all your body movements smooth and your sail adjustments gentle. If your jib and mainsheet blocks have a ratchet system fitted, switch them off to allow the sheets to run easily.

STRONG WINDS

In strong winds there is considerable power in the sails on a reach and the forward pressure will constantly force the leeward bow down.

CREW WEIGHT

The helmsman should position themselves as far back as possible. So should the crew: when trapezing, one foot will be aft of the rear beam. They should lower themselves on the trapeze adjuster to be horizontal. The crew may also choose to use the restraining line to aid stability.

If you are the helmsman, you will really need to work hard to keep the windward hull out of the water, avoiding nose dives and steering through waves. You will be sitting against the rear beam, sitting out hard and sheeting hard so that the leeward hull is always above the surface of the water.

You will be sailing on a knife edge, so watch out for the approaching gust on the water, be ready to ease the sheet as soon as it hits and avoid the sudden lifting of a hull which may cause you to take extreme actions that might drop the crew in the water.

AIRFLOW

Keep the sails set to the telltales as much as possible. If your catamaran is going to capsize: spill wind from the mainsail. If at any point the cat is hit by a gust and the acceleration causes the leeward bow to bury, threatening a 'cartwheel', ease out the jib to reduce the pressure and, if necessary, reduce the power in the mainsail. You will notice that the tremendous acceleration and deceleration will change the apparent wind considerably, so you may need to make rapid sail adjustments. If constantly overpowered: ease the traveller more.

TECHNIQUE

Concentrate on keeping the catamaran 'wound up' and going at full speed. Don't use too much rudder but look out for waves that might stop the cat: luff a little as the bow hits a trough, climb the back of the next wave, then bear away on the crest.

When a gust hits, ease the sails slightly and then pull them back in when your catamaran is up to speed. Make sure the crew is secure and has their weight out and as far back as possible.

Reaching in strong winds: the crew is on the trapeze to keep the cat level, and both helm and crew are well back to counteract any tendency to nose dive

REACHING TROUBLESHOOTING

Problem	Cause	Solution
Difficulty controlling hull height	Excessive twist in mainsail leech	Ease traveller and sheet in mainsheet
Lack of power / speed	Over or under sheeted or jib slot incorrect	Check telltales are flowing correctly on both main and jib
Nose diving of leeward hull	Weight distribution or traveller position incorrect	More crew weight aft, ease traveller, open slot between mainsail and jib
Excessive rudder noise / turbulence	Rudder alignment incorrect or crew weight too far aft	Check rudder alignment ashore Adjust weight distribution Check mainsail is not oversheeted

No boat can sail straight into the wind: that is from A to B in the diagram. If you try, the wind will simply pass either side of the sail and the cat will be blown backwards. The only way to get from A to B is to sail a zigzag course at an angle of about 45° to the wind.

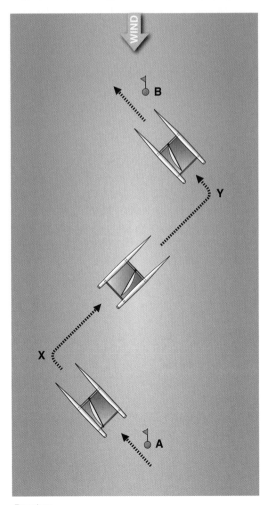

To do this you need the sails pulled right in, both the jib and mainsail. The crew will need to balance the catamaran by leaning out, possibly using the trapeze. The course sailed is a compromise between boatspeed and the shortest distance to your goal. If you point too close to the wind, your catamaran will slow down but you will get closer to your goal. If you point away from the wind, you will go faster but sail further away from your goal and travel further.

The simple way to check how close to the wind you can sail is to watch the front of your jib. With the sails pulled in, turn towards the wind until the front of the jib begins to collapse at the luff or the windward tell-tale starts to lift, then turn away from the wind until the luff stops collapsing or the windward tell-tale is lifting only intermittently. You are now sailing as close to the wind as possible without losing speed. Repeat this manoeuvre every few seconds to check your course and maintain a course on the edge of the 'no-go zone'.

If you are sailing without a jib, you will have to sail more by the feel of the catamaran, because the mainsail is fully battened and will not flap. Turn towards the wind until your cat starts to lose speed and becomes sluggish. Turn away from the wind to let it pick up speed and become responsive.

When travelling from A to B you will need to tack at X and Y. (The method of tacking is given in the next chapter.) When you tack you will pass through the 'no-go zone' before sailing off at approximately 90° to your original course.

Beating

MEDIUM WINDS

CREW WEIGHT

The position of your crew weight is important to performance when beating. Too far towards the back of the catamaran and the stern will drag in the water and the rudders will become heavy to use. Too far forward and the bows will try to keep going in a straight line whatever you do, and you will need to use a lot of rudder to change direction. With the crew weight in the correct position the stern is just out of the water with the bow cutting cleanly through the waves. If your cat has a waterline marked, keep it parallel to the water. Ideally, the helm and crew should be close together to reduce the pitching movement.

If the weight is too far forward, the bows go down and it is hard to steer	*Too far back and the transoms will drag in the water and slow you down*	*Keep the waterline level for a clean passage through the water*

AIRFLOW

When beating in average winds, pull the mainsail and jib in tight. Put the jibsheet in the jammers at position 2 (see box), but keep the mainsheet free for any adjustment. The correct tension on the mainsheet is critical and it should be set so that the leech (back) of the mainsail has a very slight twist to leeward.

In stronger winds the twist will increase and you will need more tension on the mainsheet. In lighter winds less twist is generated so you will need less mainsheet tension to hold the leech straight.

The telltales provide a good indication that you have achieved the right sail balance. When the windward telltale on the jib stalls, the top windward telltale on the mainsail should also stall. This means both sails are stalling together, which is ideal.

If the main is sheeted too tight, the leech hooks to windward	*With too little sheet tension, the leech is too open for efficiency*	*Here the mainsheet tension is just right, giving a straight leech*

Marking The Sheets

It is well worth marking the principal sheeting positions with a waterproof pen. To do this, find a sheltered part of the beach and turn the catamaran head to wind. Then:

1. Make sure the jib sheeting position of the blocks is equal on both sides of the cat relative to the main beam.
2. Sheet the jib hard on one side and mark the sheet with a waterproof pen where it passes through the camcleat on the block.
3. Measure the distance between the jib clew and the block.
4. Move the jib to the other side and cleat it so the distance is the same and make a mark at the new camcleat.

You now have the hardest tension you will need on each sheet. Ideally at this stage you should go sailing in a force 4 and test the positions.

5. Put the sheets back in the cams at the black marks and mark two further points at 10 cm intervals on each sheet as you release them. Treat these marks as reference points 1, 2, 3, to sheet tension when sailing.

On the mainsheet with its large purchase system a small sheet adjustment makes an even smaller sail adjustment although that can have quite a substantial sail shape effect.

On the beach, with the catamaran head to wind, tension the main luff downhaul, tension the mainsheet and walk back about three metres. View the mainsail leech and tension the mainsheet until the top section of the sails leech lines up with the mast. Mark the sheet at the point it exits the cam cleat, now pull on maximum sheet tension and mark the sheet again. These are your two sheet tension reference points when sailing up-wind relating to leech twist.

Marking the jibsheet

Marking the mainsheet

TECHNIQUE

On a beat, the wind creates the maximum amount of sideways force: to resist this, make sure the boards (if fitted) are right down. Catamarans without boards should have as much of the leeward hull as possible immersed in the water. Keeping the windward hull just kissing the water gives maximum boatspeed in most wind conditions.

No sailing boat is 100% efficient: when beating to windward your catamaran will always make a certain amount of sideways slip, or leeway. When planning your zig-zag route against the wind you must allow for this when passing obstructions, also allowing for any tide or current.

Gusts

Nothing about the wind is constant. Gusts can often be seen on the water as dark moving patches.

As a gust hits you, your cat will accelerate under the increased power and you may need to lean out further. If the gust is strong enough to lift the windward hull out of the water, increase leverage by trapezing or leaning out or ease the mainsheet to spill some wind from the sail. Try to do this without altering course, e.g., pointing the catamaran towards the wind (luffing), as this will stall both sails and slow you down.

Lulls

If there are gusts there are also likely to be lulls. Make sure that you re-balance and trim your cat as it slows down and, if necessary, ease out a few centimetres of mainsheet to take advantage of the conditions and keep the sails powered up.

Windshifts

The wind changes in direction as well as strength. Some changes are small while others are quite dramatic, sometimes as much as 20° - 30° and can last much longer. Obviously you will need to adjust your course to take advantage of each windshift.

In light winds get as far forwards as you can to keep the waterline covered

On the beat, a catamaran sails most efficiently with one hull just kissing the water

This may look exciting, but it is not the fastest way to sail! Keep the windward hull just clipping the wave tops

LIGHT WINDS

CREW WEIGHT

The crew should be well forward, curled around the mast with their elbow on the beam to windward. The helmsman should be on the weather deck in front of the shroud. The idea is to keep the waterline constantly covered; with a non-centreboard catamaran, the cat should be sailed bow down.

AIRFLOW

Use the top leeward telltale of the mainsail as a guide. It should stream across the back of the sail at all times. If you over-tension the mainsheet, the sail will hook and the telltale will stall and stop flowing horizontally.

The leech of the jib must remain open (between positions 1 and 2) so that the flow of air between the jib and the mainsail (the slot) is not choked (too tight).

It is essential that, as the windspeed increases, both the mainsheet and jibsheet are tensioned to maintain leech position and, as the pressure decreases, the sheets are eased to prevent oversheeting the leech. For the jibsheet you may be talking about only 2-3 cm and for the mainsheet 10-20 cm.

The helmsman will be fine-tuning the direction of the cat all the time, sailing with the luff of the jib just about to back. You can afford to 'pinch' a bit in a gust, but you must keep your cat moving in the lulls.

Be careful not to pull the jib in too tight, because this will destroy the sail shape and narrow the slot between the jib and mainsail. The mainsheet tension should be just sufficient to bring the leech almost in line with the centreline of the cat. Too much tension and the mainsheet will cause the leech to hook over to the windward side in the light winds – a sure way of losing speed.

TECHNIQUE

Sail the catamaran free – do not 'pinch' too close to the wind. It is imperative that you keep your cat moving to give steerage and keep the air flowing over the sails.

STRONG WINDS

The method of sailing to windward in strong winds varies according to your total crew weight. Heavy crews can sail free and power along while lighter crews will need to luff up into the wind slightly, spilling wind and going slower – but pointing higher.

CREW WEIGHT

Arrange your weight to prevent the catamaran pitching; usually this means placing the crew just behind the shrouds.

AIRFLOW

Initially have both sails in tight. The stronger the wind the more the leech of the mainsail will try to fall away and the more mainsheet tension is needed to close it. The jib is pulled into position 3. As you start to become overpowered, ease out the mainsheet to spill wind and to keep the windward hull kissing the wave tops.

In very strong winds the amount you can ease the mainsheet is restricted by the air flowing through the slot between main and jib, which stops the fully-battened mainsail from spilling wind. This can also make the mast bend in reverse and rotate to windward, which could lead to it breaking.

The solution is to first ease the jib slightly to open the slot between the sails, or move the jib traveller

Keep the cat almost flat, with the windward hull just kissing the water

out (if fitted), followed by easing the mainsheet traveller a little and sheeting the mainsail in as tight as possible. This effectively means that the mainsail is driving the catamaran to windward with the jib luffing slightly.

TECHNIQUE

Continually reset the sails for maximum power. Watch out for waves and feed the catamaran over them moving your weight to assist the cat's passage through the water. If you are too far forward the main beam will catch the waves while if you are too far back the bow will slam and the transom will drag.

Keep the boards fully down (if fitted) unless continually overpowered in which case raise them partially until you have good upwind control

If you have boards (foils), push them right down on the beat to minimise leeway

BEATING TROUBLESHOOTING

Problem	Cause	Solution
The catamaran has no power	The sails are not set correctly	Check the sails are set correctly from the telltales
The catamaran will not sail close to the wind	The traveller line is not pulled in enough	Pull the traveller line in
The rudders feel 'heavy' or difficulty in steering	The crew positions are not distributed correctly or the mainsail is oversheeted	Adjust crew positions to balance the blade Interpret the mainsail telltales and leech twist correctly
The catamaran travels slowly and is sluggish to steer	Pointing too close to the wind	Bear off slightly so that the top set of telltales are streaming on both sides of the sail
The catamaran is sailing fast through the water, but not making much windward progress	Pointing too far off the wind	Head up a bit so that the top set of telltales are streaming on both sides of the sail
The windward hull is way out of the water	There is too much power in the sail or the crew weight is not far out enough	Increase downhaul tension Ease the mainsheet Point closer into the wind Increase weight / leverage on the windward hull

Tacking a catamaran is not like tacking a dinghy and it is a good idea to practise the sequence on land, so you are familiar with the necessary movements.

PRACTISING ON LAND

Place the catamaran on a soft surface such as grass or sand, and connect the rudder assembly. With the sails down, clip the mainsheet to the main halyard. Both helm and crew should be sitting on one side of the cat, imagining that they are beating against the wind with the sails sheeted fully in.

HELMSMAN

- Sit on one side of the catamaran with your feet under the toestraps, your front hand (nearest the bow) holding the mainsheet and your back hand holding the tiller extension in a dagger grip on your shoulder.
- Fix in your mind that you are beating against the wind, with the sails sheeted in, and that you are going to tack.
- Check that the cat is 'sailing' as close to the wind as possible, the sails pulled in, traveller in, boards down (if fitted).
- Give the order "Ready to tack", check the sailing area and move your feet, so that your back leg is bent under your front leg outside the toestraps.
- Place the spare mainsheet in the centre of the trampoline and prepare to tack.
- Saying "Lee-o", initiate the turning of the catamaran by pushing the tiller extension away until the rudders are at 45° to the hulls. This should be done in a firm steady movement rather like sailing a cruiser or driving a big lorry, not too gently or too violently.

- Wait until the mainsail and bows 'point into the wind', then start to move across the cat by rolling onto the knee of your back leg, and face towards the back of the catamaran.
- Pass the tiller extension around the back of the mainsheet falls. At this point you should be kneeling, facing backwards, rudders still at 45°.
- Easing the mainsheet slightly when head to wind will help reset the mainsail on the new tack.
- Change hands on the tiller extension (behind the mainsheet falls) and mainsheet and move to the new hull.
- Centralise your rudders when the mainsail battens have 'popped' and the sails have settled on the new tack.

CREW

Because the catamaran is sailing into the wind the crew will have to sheet the jib in fully.

- When the helmsman calls "Ready to tack" check the sailing area, call "All clear" (if it is!) and prepare to cross the catamaran by tucking your front leg under your back leg.

- As the cat turns move to the centre, facing forward on your knees, and uncleat the jibsheet.
- Keep an eye on the jib: you are waiting for the wind to push on the reverse side of the sail and the main to cross to the new side.
- At the point when the jib fills on the reverse side prepare to free the jibsheet, move to the new side and sheet in. This will ensure the jib flaps as little as possible between tacks. If in doubt, do not release the jib until you see or hear the mainsail battens pop to the new side.
- When tacking catamarans with limited hull buoyancy in the bow and stern it is often better to move directly to the new side well before the tack is completed.

1 Start in your normal beating position

2 The helmsman pushes the tiller away until the rudders are at 45° to the hulls

3 Start to move across the cat keeping the tiller hard over

4 Change hands on the tiller extension and mainsheet

5 Swivel the tiller extension over while maintaining the position of the rudders

6 Establish yourself on the new side and straighten up

TACKING IN MEDIUM WINDS

Follow the procedure practised on shore (above).

A medium-wind tack should be a simple, fast and efficient turn which leaves the catamaran with good speed when settled on the new windward course. Sheet the sails fully, get up some speed and initiate the turn by turning the rudder to 45° before crossing the catamaran. Move your legs as described for tacking practise on land, so that your body crosses the catamaran smoothly.

It is helpful to release the mainsheet by a few centimetres in the middle of the tack to help the battens flick over. When you sheet the mainsail back in, your catamaran will accelerate away on its new course.

When sailing single handed, without a jib to help you tack or assist your mainsail airflow, you should turn a few degrees more than when sailing with a jib:

- Ease the mainsheet as you pass head to wind, creating more twist in the head of the sail to encourage airflow on the new tack, sheeting in smoothly as you accelerate away.
- Once airflow is established on the new tack, head the catamaran back onto the edge of the 'no go zone'.

1 Start in your normal beating position

2 The helmsman pushes the tiller away...

3 ...until the rudders are at 45° to the hulls

4 Start to move across the cat keeping the tiller hard over

5 Change hands on the tiller extension and mainsheet

6 Straighten up and sail off on the new tack

TACKING IN LIGHT WINDS

When sailing in light winds, you must move smoothly to keep your catamaran moving and to encourage air to flow over the sails for as long as possible.

HELMSMAN

- Apply smooth but firm pressure on the helm and don't straighten up until the tack is complete. Keep the mainsheet tension to help drive the cat up to the wind. To help spin the catamaran, stay on the windward side a little longer.
- Move to the rear of the cat and pass the tiller extension behind the mainsheet, taking care not to change the rudder angle. It is important to release the sheet as the cat passes through the eye of the wind. Let out approximately 60 cm of sheet and efficently flick the clew (holding the mainsheet falls near the sail) to ensure battens pop across in one movement.
- As the new course is taken up: tension the mainsheet as the catamaran accelerates (no sudden movement) and adjust it so that the air reattaches and flows across the back of both sails.
- Move your weight forward as smoothly as possible.

CREW

- Hold the sheet in the cleat on the order "Ready about" and prepare to cross the cat.
- Ensure that the excess sheet is clear and in front (forward) of your body position.
- On "Lee-o", do not release the sheet but watch the jib shape. As you see the jib start to back, release the old sheet and start sheeting in the new one. (By backing the jib for longer you help push the bow around to ensure the tack is completed but reduce acceleration.)
- Move your weight forward on the new side and check the mast has rotated.
- Re-tension the jibsheet to its mark position as the catamaran accelerates.

TACKING IN STRONG WINDS

Strong-wind tacking also demands good timing and boatspeed. You may have eased the mainsail to prevent capsizing when sailing to windward; this will cause drag if the sail is allowed to flog as the catamaran moves through the tack, so remember to sheet in as you enter the 'no-go zone' but be ready to ease out as you reach head to wind. Waves can also stop the bows turning so look ahead and select your spot to tack.

HELMSMAN

- Look ahead for a smoother patch of water.
- Call "Ready about". As the crew comes off the trapeze, start to turn. Do not release the mainsheet – the power is needed to push the stern around. If not already fully sheeted in, pull in the extra mainsheet as you start the tack then, as the bows approach head to wind, ease the sheet in preparation for lining up on new tack.
- Move smoothly to the centre of the catamaran as the cat rotates head to wind, maintaining pressure on the helm, while passing the extension across to the new side, exchanging hands on both tiller extension and mainsheet and making sure that you maintain the turning pressure on the rudders.
- Just as the catamaran passes through the wind, release some mainsheet tension, to aid the battens 'popping' across, by which time you should be nearly across the cat, with the sheet in your forward hand.
- Straighten the helm as the mainsail powers up and the crew starts to move out onto the trapeze wire, sheeting in at the same time.

CREW

- On the command "Ready about", maintain tension on the jibsheet and check the loose sheet is ready to run.
- On "Lee-o", come onto the hull and start crossing the catamaran just as the bow enters the 'no-go zone'. As you get better you should delay coming off the trapeze for as long as possible.
- Watch the wind indicator and 'feel' the cat's progress through the wind. Ideally you should release the jib just as it backs, but you may need to continue backing it if the turn is too slow or the catamaran needs additional help in turning.
- When satisfied the mainsail has crossed, release the old sheet and, as quickly as possible, pull in the new sheet. Hook on to the trapeze and go out. The cat cannot gain speed until you have completed the tack.

A tip, when tacking without a jib in strong winds, is to ease the traveller off the centre to prevent the catamaran spinning back into the wind on the new tack.

In strong winds you need to prepare for your tack, ideally in a smoother patch of water

STOPPING HEAD TO WIND

If you get held head to wind when tacking, you will have to do a 'three-point-turn'. You will only get stopped (in irons) if speed is lost because:

- A rogue wave has hit the catamaran – the helmsman chose a bad place to tack.
- The rudders have been released half-way through the tack, reducing the turning rate.
- Maximum tension was not kept on the mainsheet, allowing the main to flog.
- The team moved too quickly across catamaran.
- The jibsheet was released too soon.

If you fail a tack, you will now be going backwards. To get going again on the new tack:

- Sheet the jib back in.
- Turn the rudders towards the direction you want the back of the cat to go: normally opposite to when you started the tack.
- Release a lot of mainsheet and traveller.
- When you have swung round onto the course for the new tack, centralise the rudders, release the jibsheet and sheet in on the new side.
- Only now can you pull in the traveller line, then the mainsheet and accelerate away on the new tack.

A photo sequence of this can be found on p41.

TACKING TROUBLESHOOTING

Problem	Cause	Solution
The catamaran does not turn head to wind	Not tightening the mainsheet fully before the tack	Sheet the mainsheet in fully before starting the tack
The catamaran is slow in tacking	Not sailing on the edge of the 'no-go zone'	Sail closer to the wind before tacking
	Moving too quickly across the cat	Don't start to move across until the bows are head to wind
The catamaran is sailing too slowly before the tack	Sailing inside the 'no-go zone'	Bear away slightly and get up speed before tacking
The catamaran loses unacceptable speed in the turn	Not holding the rudder at 45° throughout the tack	Keep the rudder at 45° throughout the tack
The catamaran is slow to reach head to wind	The traveller is off centre	Centre the traveller before the tack
The catamaran loses speed in the turn	Allowing the mainsheet to run out as you tack	Only release the mainsheet slighly, once in the 'no-go zone', during the tack
Loss of speed into the tack	Letting go of the jib too early, so that it flaps	Keep the jib on its original side until the mainsail battens have popped
The catamaran is slow to accelerate on the new tack	Keeping the jib aback too long	Release the jib earlier

All catamarans can run with the wind directly behind them but, because of their incredible speed in relation to the wind's strength, it is generally far more efficient to 'tack' downwind in a zig-zag fashion (rather like beating against the wind). You will soon find that there is an optimum angle for sailing downwind, just as there is for sailing upwind. This angle is approximately 90° to the apparent wind and will vary depending on a variety of conditions and type of catamaran.

APPARENT WIND

The word 'apparent' is a good way of describing the direction of the wind indicated by your wind indicator or flag when your catamaran is travelling at speed. When a boat is at rest, the direction of the wind indicator is an indication of the true direction of the wind, but as the catamaran accelerates its forward movement generates, in effect, a second wind blowing from the front. This second wind and the real wind combine to become the apparent wind.

This can be likened to putting your hand out of a car window when the car is moving: although the true wind may be blowing across the car it will feel as though the wind is blowing from the front because the car is travelling forward through the air.

Apparent wind enables a catamaran to 'tack' downwind at speed. As a starting point, the downwind indicator should be kept at around 90° to the cat.

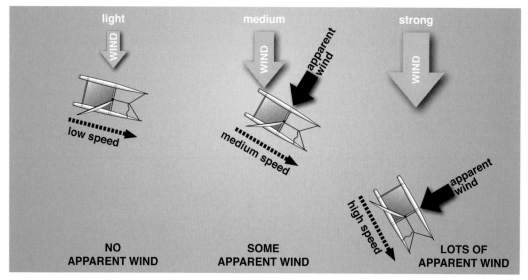

How apparent wind is generated for downwind sailing

MEDIUM WINDS

CREW WEIGHT

Crew weight will need to be distributed evenly between the two hulls. In moderate conditions this often means that the helm and crew are positioned with the helm sitting on the hull deck and crew by the mast, facing forward as if reaching. As the wind increases the crew may need to move aft and towards the windward side to help trim the hulls and balance the catamaran with the helm moving aft down the deck.

Downwind the fore-and-aft trim is very sensitive. Normally you should try to keep the cat level and the transom just out of the water. In lighter winds move further forward, while in strong winds you may both need to move back dramatically to prevent the bows digging in.

AIRFLOW

In medium winds you will need to ease the traveller right out and ease the mainsheet until the sail just touches the shrouds – any further than this and the sail will deform around the shrouds and its aerodynamic properties will be lost. Set the traveller right out to reduce the twist in the leech (back edge) of the sail and ease the jibsheet until the luff (front) of the jib is about to flap. Now your sails are set for downwind sailing.

Running in medium winds: note that the traveller is as far across as it will go, allowing the helmsman to control the shape of the sail with the mainsheet

TECHNIQUE

When sailing downwind, the board position is raised: the exact amount depending on the shape and type of catamaran. Too much board down can make the hull nose dive, too little and steering is compromised.

The shortest distance between points A and B in the diagram overleaf is a straight line downwind, but for catamarans (as with other high performance boats) this is not the quickest way. Instead you should keep the bridle wire wind indicator at around 90° to the catamaran, giving you a zig-zag course to point B, gybing occasionally.

The stronger the wind the faster the catamaran will go, and the stronger the apparent wind becomes relative to the real wind, meaning that the apparent wind moves forward. This means that you can sail downwind on a broader angle (see overleaf, left).

You should also use the top, leeward telltale on the mainsail. The aim is to get maximum leeway without stalling the air flowing over the sails: that is, letting the telltale drop. As soon as it does drop, the flow of wind over the back of the sail will have broken down and the only way of recovering it is to head up, creating airflow and causing the catamaran to accelerate.

As the speed builds, the apparent wind will come forward, flow will build up over the mainsail again and you can slowly bear away – but not too far or the sail will stall again and the whole process has to be repeated (see overleaf, right).

Downwind sailing does, therefore, involve quite substantial changes in direction, particularly for the inexperienced as you can repeatedly stall out and have to head up to accelerate again. As experience and feel increase, the deviations become less and less until the vital knife-edge is found where the mainsail never stalls out.

The crew plays a major role, working with the helm to keep the telltales parallel; this includes the jib, and quickly adjusting to any change in direction

PART 2

72

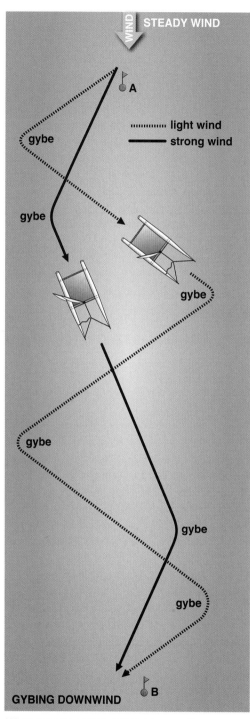

STEADY WIND

WIND

● A

.... light wind
———— strong wind

gybe

gybe

gybe

gybe

gybe

gybe

gybe

GYBING DOWNWIND

● B

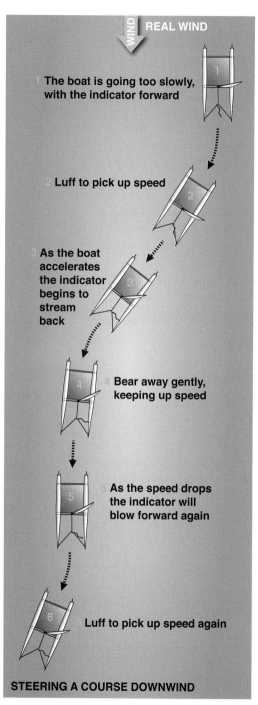

REAL WIND

WIND

1 The boat is going too slowly, with the indicator forward

2 Luff to pick up speed

3 As the boat accelerates the indicator begins to stream back

4 Bear away gently, keeping up speed

5 As the speed drops the indicator will blow forward again

6 Luff to pick up speed again

STEERING A COURSE DOWNWIND

When you are sailing fast in a breeze the apparent wind moves forward, so you can aim more directly for your goal while still keeping the wind indicator at approximately 90° to the cat

Since a cat sails most efficiently with the wind indicator at approximately 90° to the cat, you should always steer to keep it at that angle. You will find that as you accelerate you can bear away, but if you lose speed you will have to luff up again

of the catamaran or the wind. It is vitally important to hook on to the new wind direction over the sail and, as the helm bears away, ease the jibsheet gently responding to the change of direction.

The helmsman may well ask "What direction am I going to go in when I gybe?" If they are on a true downwind course, with the apparent wind at right angles to the catamaran, the crew can look straight down the beams to give a good guide to the heading of the next course.

Gusts

When a gust hits the sails, your catamaran will immediately accelerate, initially causing the bows to bury. React by moving your weight aft and by keeping both hulls in the water.

Also, if you look at the bridle wire wind indicator, it will be streaming towards the stern rather than at 90°, because the apparent wind has increased. Turn away from the wind to bring the indicator back to approximately 90°.

If, at any point, the gusts become severe and the bow really buries, react by releasing the jibsheet, to reduce the load on the bow and help depower the mainsail.

Lulls

When the wind gets lighter the catamaran will slow down and the apparent wind will decrease in strength. This will allow the true wind direction to take over and the bridle wire wind indicator will start to stream forward of 90°.

If you do not react by turning the cat back towards the wind to get the indicator streaming at 90° to the cat again, the sails will stall and your catamaran will slow down even more.

Windshifts

If, when sailing downwind, a windshift forces you to steer further away from your goal, then gybe. If the windshift takes you nearer to your goal, then use it to your advantage, but do not sail too far before gybing to reach your destination.

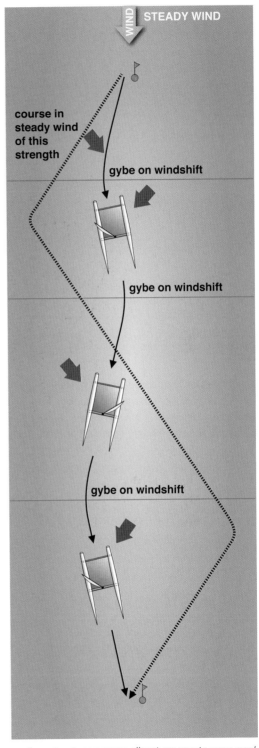

WIND | STEADY WIND

course in steady wind of this strength

gybe on windshift

gybe on windshift

gybe on windshift

If there are windshifts, gybe on them to steer a more direct course to your goal.
You may gybe more frequently than you would in steady wind, but it's worth it

SUMMING UP

Sailing downwind in catamarans is basically a series of broad reaches keeping the wind indicator at approximately 90° to the cat. Because the wind varies slightly in strength and apparent direction, the course sailed will not be straight, but a meandering line which is always around 90° to the direction of the apparent wind.

The most effective downwind sailing angle will vary between classes but the principle stays the same.

LIGHT WINDS

CREW WEIGHT

As always in light winds, move as smoothly as possible to avoid disturbing the air flowing over the sails.

By sitting forward of the hull balance point you will bring the transom out of the water and depress the bows slightly. To balance the catamaran the crew and helmsman should be positioned one on each hull. The helm should be on the windward hull, the crew on the leeward hull close to the main beam.

AIRFLOW

Allow the sails to be as far forward as possible. The crew can manually hold the jib out with their free hand, keep the mast in its fully rotated position with the foot and stabilise the mainsail with the free hand.

In light winds, keep the cat level by sitting one on either hull, well forward to stop the transoms digging in the water

TECHNIQUE

In light winds it is very easy to stall the sails. Try pointing a little higher into the wind than usual to get your catamaran moving before bearing away downwind. In the very lightest winds it sometimes pays to sail almost dead downwind in some types of catamarans as the amount of apparent wind created is minimal.

STRONG WINDS

CREW WEIGHT

Sit near the stern to keep the cat level, fore-and-aft. At these speeds, if the bows dip under the water, the catamaran may cartwheel or pitchpole unless the crew reacts immediately by moving further back.

By holding the catamaran on an even keel, the downward pressure on the bow is shared between both hulls. Generally the crew will be on the windward hull and as far aft as possible.

AIRFLOW

Some mainsheet tension is needed to stop the sail distorting around the shroud.

Because the crew is on the windward side, the jib is controlled through the jibsheet block. If, owing to gusts or waves, the bow begins to bury, you should immediately release the jib to reduce the pressure on the bow. As soon as the bow has popped back up, sheet the jib back in to maintain boatspeed. Often it is only the initial strength of the gust that forces the bow down.

When conditions are extreme and your catamaran is continually tripping over itself, head further downwind, depower the mainsail by sheeting it in and pulling in the traveller a little. This will spoil the airflow and decrease the pressure on the bows. On lower aspect cats (Hobie 16 or similar) by easing the mainsail fully you allow the top of the leach to blow forward, reducing the downward pressure.

TECHNIQUE

Downwind in a very strong wind, the technique may be more about prevention and control than ultimate speed.

Two typical problems are cartwheeling and pitchpoling (see photo sequences overleaf).

Cartwheeling

When the bow of one hull is forced down, either by the power in the sails or by a wave stopping the catamaran, you may find yourself cartwheeling. The effect is to pivot the cat up and over on the point of the bow, throwing the helm and crew forward into the sail or water. The experience can be quite exhilarating! But take care. (See overleaf, top.)

To reduce the chance of this happening, get the crew to keep an eye on the bow; when they see it starting to bury, release the jibsheet to reduce the pressure on the bow. On a reach the helmsman can help by easing the mainsail. Do not bear away or luff up as this will only aggravate the situation.

Cartwheeling can also be caused by bearing away without easing the sheets, or not raising the boards, which causes pressure on the leeward bow so, when bearing away in strong winds, ease jib, main, traveller, and raise the boards (if fitted).

Pitchpoling

Pitchpoling occurs when both hulls are forced under the water at the same time, causing the catamaran to stop very abruptly and lifting the stern end right out of the water and over. This normally happens only on windy days with severe gusts, when the cat trips over itself going downwind (a cat rarely pitchpoles on a reach and even more rarely on a beat). (See overleaf, bottom.)

To prevent pitchpoling, keep your catamaran level on the water for more bow buoyancy, turn the cat further downwind and pull in the mainsail to de-power the rig or, as highlighted before, on low-aspect cats, release the mainsheet to allow the leech to blow forward. If the bow starts to go down, release the jib promptly.

Going downwind in strong winds is where the excitement starts

PART 2

75

Cartwheeling

1 The leeward bow goes down

2 And carries on down

3 By releasing the jib and mainsheet

4 Things begin to recover and the bow begins to come up again

Pitchpoling

1 If both bows go down

2 The cat will start pitchpoling

3 And there is only one way it is going to end...

4 You can cling on all you like

5 It's going...

6 All the way

DOWNWIND TROUBLESHOOTING

Problem	Cause	Solution
Lack of speed and power	The sail is stalling because the mainsail is in too tight	Ease the mainsail
Lack of performance	Too little air is being forced over the back of the mainsail and the jib is stalling because it is out too far	Pull in the jib and read the telltales to set the slot between the two sails
Lack of performance or mast inverting	The air cannot flow over the back of the mainsail because the jib is in too tight	Ease the jib to reset the slot between the two sails
Hulls continually want to nose dive cartwheel	Too much twist in the mainsail because the traveller is on the centreline of the rear beam making the mainsail less efficient	Ease the traveller to reduce sail twist
The battens are distorted round the shroud	The mainsail is out too far	Pull in the mainsheet to set the battens off the shroud
The bow is in the air and the transom is dragging	The crew weight is too far back	Move forward
The catamaran is out of balance	The crew weight is all on one side	Distribute crew weight more evenly across the platform
The catamaran loses speed as you turn downwind	The sails are stalled because the apparent wind is too far aft	Head up until the bridle wire wind indicator is approximately 90°
The catamaran is not heading as far downwind as it could	You are not bearing away in relation to the apparent wind angle	Bear away until the bridle wire wind indicator is approximately 90°
The bow is burying under the water	The crew weight is too far forward or the sails are set incorrectly	Move the weight aft and / or ease the jib tension

GYBING

The best thing about gybing is that, unlike tacking, you can guarantee it will take place! However, gybing a catamaran requires a large amount of sea room and full boat control. Practise first on the beach without sails before trying it on the water.

PRACTISING ON LAND

HELMSMAN

- Steer the catamaran onto a downwind course with the bridle wire wind indicator at 90° across the cat. The sails should be set as far out as possible, the jib so it is not quite flapping, the mainsail almost touching the shroud and the traveller right out. The boards (if fitted) should be 75% up.
- Prepare to gybe by tucking your back leg under the front as for tacking and say "Stand by to gybe".
- Initiate the turn by pulling the tiller towards you and move immediately across the catamaran on your knees, facing backwards, to the other hull.
- Keeping the turn on, move the tiller over to the new side behind the mainsheet, change hands and put your new front hand on the falls of the mainsheet.
- Wait for the sail to cross, centralise the rudders and check the movement of the mainsheet falls before letting them cross to the new side (this 'pops' the battens on the new side).
- Sit down, look forward and bring the catamaran back onto a downwind course with the bridle wire wind indicator at 90° across the cat.

CREW

- Set the jib correctly and wait for the order to gybe.
- When the helm gives the command "Stand by to gybe", check the sailing area and, if all is well, answer "All clear".
- Tuck your front leg in under your back leg and tidy away the jibsheets forward of your body.
- As the catamaran turns further downwind, move to the middle of the cat and watch for the jib to collapse.
- As this happens, cross the jib to the new side; the mainsail will follow soon after.
- Reposition yourself to balance the catamaran and trim the hulls fore-and-aft.

1 Steer downwind and get ready to gybe

2 Prepare to cross the cat

3 Steer the cat around and get ready to change hands

4 Change hands on the tiller and mainsheet in preparation for the sail to cross

5 Control the mainsheet falls as they cross, popping the battens on the new side

6 Sail away on the new gybe

GYBING IN MEDIUM WINDS

Follow the procedure you have practised ashore (above).

1 Steer downwind and get ready to gybe

2 Start turning the cat

3 Swap hands

4 Control the mainsail falls as they cross

5 Check the mainsheet to pop the battens on the new side

6 Sail away on the new gybe

When gybing single handed, maintaining mainsail airflow is critical before and after the gybe. Heading up a little more after the gybe will help re-attach the airflow before bearing away onto the new downwind course.

GYBING IN LIGHT WINDS

As for tacking, the secret of gybing in light airs is smoothness of movement by both helmsman and crew. Keep your weight right forward and settle onto the new course quickly.

HELMSMAN

- Warn the crew.
- Begin the turn and move towards the rear beam as you start to cross the platform, passing the extension to the new windward side.
- Let the wind do the work in passing the mainsail across. Take the falls of the mainsheet just below the clew, follow the sail across and, just after it passes the centre, check the mainsheet falls to 'pop' the battens onto the new gybe.
- Smoothly return to the front of the cat and 'hook on' to the new wind flowing over the sails.

CREW

You should be sitting on the lee hull, near the main beam, holding the jib sheet out to set the jib.

- Move smoothly across the catamaran to a similar position on the other side as the jib collapses and feed the jibsheet through on to the new side.
- Quickly get the jib telltales flowing parallel over the sail on the new side.

GYBING IN STRONG WINDS

The aim is to gybe at maximum speed (rather than when accelerating), with the rudders deep in the water. Look to get maximum speed up before you gybe, selecting flat water or brief lull while your catamaran is still travelling fast. This reduces the apparent wind and makes the manoeuvre less violent.

In really windy weather, the crew will be well aft in the catamaran and to windward, close to the helmsman.

HELMSMAN

- Move to the back of the catamaran and prepare to gybe.
- Initiate the turn by gently pulling the tiller extension towards you (since you are going fast you need less rudder movement to turn).
- Move across the cat on your knees and change hands as already described.
- As the mainsail becomes ineffective pull the mainsheet falls to the centreline of the cat and check their movement as they cross to the other side (the cat should be pointing downwind).
- As you check the mainsheet falls, centralise the rudders. In extreme conditions compensate for the kick of the mainsheet by over-compensating on the helm and turning the catamaran downwind.
- Once you have completed the gybe look forward, recover the mainsheet and return to downwind sailing using the downwind telltales.

CREW

The crew does not have a great influence on gybing speed. They should aim to keep weight central and ensure the jib is quickly filled on the new gybe. Take care not to lose balance in the turn and advise the helm of any obstructions.

GYBING TROUBLESHOOTING

Problem	Cause	Solution
You lose speed in the gybe	The sails are not set correctly	Reset the sails to the downwind sailing angle
The gybe is prolonged and possibly violent	The sails are too far out	Reset the sails to the downwind sailing angle
You lose speed in the turn and the mainsail crosses more violently	The cat is heading too far downwind (stalled) just before the gybe	Start the turn when sailing higher, with the bridle wire wind indicator at 90° and your cat at a maximum speed
You start to nose dive or lose steering	The cat is not balanced or trimmed correctly	Reinstate C.A.T control
You lose control of the catamaran via the steering	The gybe was not initiated before crossing the platform	Initiate the gybe before crossing the platform
You lose the continuous turn as you move from one hull to the other and the catamaran slows	Straightening the rudders too early	Keep the turn initiated until the gybe is completed
The mainsheet falls hit you or you struggle to change hands smoothly	Not changing hands before the mainsail crosses	Change hands before the mainsail crosses the cat
The catamaran wants to screw up into the wind after the manoeuvre	Not 'checking' the mainsheet falls as they cross	'Check' the mainsheet falls as the mainsheet crosses the cat
The catamaran sails off in the wrong direction, accelerates alarmingly or stalls downwind	Not looking forward after completing the gybe to bring the cat back onto a downwind course	Keep an eye on where you are heading so you steer in the correct direction when the gybe is completed
The catamaran screws up into the wind and throws the crew off balance	Not straightening the rudders immediately after the mainsail crosses	Straighten the rudders immediately after the mainsail crosses

Trapezing is a method of extending your body weight out further from the side of the catamaran to give more righting effect. This allows you to harness more wind without the likelihood of capsizing and hence increase your boatspeed. What's more, out on the trapeze, the feeling of power and speed is exhilarating!

THE HARNESS

The harness is rather like a nappy with a back support. It needs to be strapped firmly around your hips and adjusted at the shoulder straps so that your back is fully supported when in the trapezing position.

There are various styles of harness, so personal preference means trying different types before you buy. Most modern trapezes are fitted with a 'quick release hook system' to prevent accidental entanglement and are recommended to all sailors.

THE TRAPEZE WIRES

The trapeze wires are attached high up the mast and run down either side of the mast to a shock-cord restraining line. At the bottom end of each wire is a 'trapeze ring' and an adjustable line. The hook of your harness connects to the trapeze ring and the trapezing height is altered by the trapeze adjusting line or similar.

A strong, comfortable, well-fitting trapeze harness is essential equipment

The trapeze itself: the wire, handle, height adjustment block and ring, which is linked to the ring on the other side of the catamaran by a length of shockcord

HOW TO GET OUT THERE

It is a good idea to practise trapezing techniques on the beach before trying them afloat. Position the catamaran on some soft ground with the bows slightly raised.

- For your first trapeze session it is best to be sailing upwind. Settle into a normal sailing position with the jibsheet in your hand and your feet under the toestraps, and leaning out over the side.
- Attach your harness hook to the trapeze ring and transfer your weight on to the wire. Use your other hand for balance.
- Place one hand on the trapeze handle with the jibsheet in the other.
- Turn your body towards the back of the catamaran and put your front foot up onto the side of the gunwale (the edge of the deck).
- Push out and back to straighten your front leg and at the same time keeping your back leg slightly bent and position yourself with your feet on the side of the deck. (Always keep your forward leg straighter than your back leg to avoid being 'pulled' forward.)

- Fully extend your body, letting go of the trapeze handle with your hands and straighten your legs, front leg first.

Once you have settled into the trapezing position, check your trapezing height: to begin with you may feel more comfortable trapezing at a slightly raised angle but, as you grow in confidence, you should look to be level with the decks. If you are too high or too low, alter your height by using the adjuster line.

If you feel you are falling towards the bow, bend your back leg slightly. Your confidence will soon grow and you will then start to feel the movement of the catamaran through your feet. If foot loops are fitted they are there to secure your position in rough seas but usually you will not need them, allowing you to move your weight fore-and-aft to help trim the hull.

PART 2

83

1 Hook on to the trapeze wire

2 Move your bottom over the side

3 Put your front leg on the side of the cat

4 Push out on your front leg

5 Put your back foot on the side of the cat

6 Extend yourself fully

TRAPEZING HEIGHT

The height at which you trapeze is subject to the conditions. Ideally you should trapeze level with the deck, but in rough seas or light winds it is usually a good idea to be slightly higher.

MOONWALKING

During the learning period you will inevitably lose your balance and swing forward. Once your back foot has lost contact with the hull and you have pivoted forward on your front foot you have lost control and will end up swinging from the wire. To prevent that happening if you lose balance, be prepared to moonwalk forwards or backwards along the side of the hull until such time as you can re position yourself.

Note: The trapeze wire neutral hanging position is affected by the mast rake and hound position. On some catamarans you may find it easier to push out with the back foot first.

THE TRAPEZE RESTRAINING LINE

Sometimes your catamaran is going so fast, normally on a reach, that the power in the sails forces the bow down under the water. You need to re-trim your hulls by moving aft whilst on the trapeze, i.e., walking towards the back of the hull to a position behind or alongside the helmsman. Once there, the forward pull from the trapeze hang point can be considerable so some catamarans use a restraining line system which you can hold or clip onto for security.

As crew, start from your normal trapezing position. Place the jib sheet in your forward hand using the other hand to pick up the restraining line. Use the line to pull yourself back down the hull to balance the hull trim. You may find that you can secure the restraining line to your trapeze ring when in the most aft position.

You will now find you are trapezing too high, as you are further from the mast hanging point, so adjust the trapeze height as required. If the helm is sitting in they will need to hold the tiller extension further aft for clearance from your trapeze position.

When moving back to the normal trapeze position, first adjust the trapeze height back to normal and, when moving forward, hold onto the restraining line so as not to fall forward or start moonwalking!

The more you practise trapeze work, and moving up and down the hull, the more confident you will become.

When sailing fast on a reach, to prevent nose diving, trapeze further aft and make use of the restraining line.

Crew using the restraining line on land (top) and on the water

RETURNING TO THE CATAMARAN

If the wind drops, or you need to tack, you will have to come back onto the hull. To do this:

- First cleat the jibsheet in preparation for coming in.
- Take your feet out of any foot-loops and, bending your back leg more than your front, swing back in over the side. It is a good idea

to lift your backside over the lip of the gunwale by using your front hand on the handle.

- Once back on board, unhook the trapeze wire from your harness and return the jibsheet to your back hand ready for action.

1 Take hold of the trapeze handle   *2 Bend your legs and move in*   *3 Move your front leg into the cat*

4 Sit on the edge of the cat   *5 Shuffle further on board*   *6 Unclip the trapeze harness*

TRAPEZING SINGLE HANDED

The principles of single-handed trapezing (or trapezing as a helm) are much the same, but it is important that your catamaran is set up correctly before you push out – adjustments are not so easy when you're out on the wire!

Fix the traveller position, transfer the mainsheet to your tiller hand and, using your front hand, hook onto the trapeze wire. Push out over the side using your front hand on the trapeze handle for balance. Once out, and fully extended, transfer the main-

sheet to your forward hand. You will find the catamaran is very sensitive to your weight, fore and aft and, by using your legs, the mainsheet is surprisingly easy to pull in.

Loose sheets should be left on the trampoline and 'run' up your back leg to your tiller thumb to stop them dragging in the water. Any violent rudder movement will make it difficult for you to keep your balance, so make sure you keep the rudders straight as you go out on the trapeze or come back in.

Going out on the trapeze single handed / helming

1 From your normal position on the side deck

2 Transfer the mainsheet to your tiller hand to allow you to get the trapeze wire

3 Hook on to the trapeze wire

4 Move your bottom over the side

5 Put your front leg on the side

6 Push out

7 Put your back foot on the side

8 Take the mainsheet back in your front hand

9 Adopt your normal trapezing position

Coming in from the trapeze single handed / helming

1 Transfer the mainsheet to your tiller hand

2 Put any excess mainsheet on the trampolene

3 Begin to bend the knees

4 Sit on the side deck

5 Unclip from the trapeze

6 Adopt your normal non-trapezing position

TRAPEZING TROUBLESHOOTING

Problem	Cause	Solution
The trapeze hook unclips	Not putting your weight on the wire after hooking on	Put your weight on the trapeze hook when sliding out
All your weight is supported on your arm	Not relying on the hook, or unhooking when trapezing	Put your weight on the trapeze hook when sliding out
You lose your balance	Not keeping your leading leg straight as you move out or while you are trapezing	Always go out on your leading leg and bending your other leg and use your free hand
You feel as though you will fall back into the catamaran when slightly heeled over	Trapezing too high on the wire	Lower your trapeze height
You get knocked off by waves	Trapezing too low	Raise your trapeze height
The bows bury at speed	Trapezing too far forward	Move aft

MAN OVERBOARD!

Once you are reasonably confident about tacking, gybing and the three points of sailing, you will really want to turn on the speed.

This is when you are most likely to lose one of you over the side – maybe during an over-enthusiastic gybe, the crew losing their footing, or being caught unawares by a wave. Whatever the reason, it is essential that you can sail back without delay and pick up the unfortunate victim.

It is best to practise this in moderate winds – but remember that you are much more likely to lose someone when conditions are not quite so favourable.

- As soon as a person falls off the catamaran, note their position and release the jib so that you have only the mainsail to contend with.
- Sail off on a reach, keeping an eye on the person overboard.
- When you consider that you are far enough away, turn the catamaran downwind and gybe back towards him.
- After the gybe, pull the traveller almost right in and return to the MOB on a close reach using

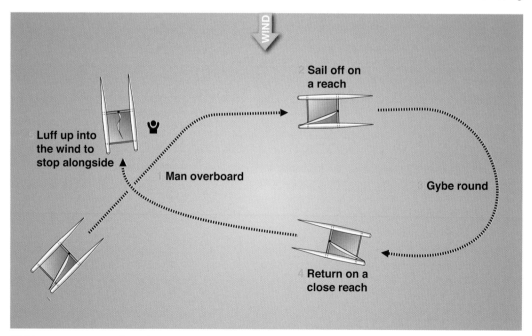

Picking up a man overboard

the mainsheet as an accelerator. Control the cat's speed back towards the crew, being sure to allow for leeway.

- On reaching the MOB, use the last of the boatspeed to point into wind so that the crew ends up alongside the windward hull, by the shroud.

- Release the traveller and mainsheet, hold the rudders over (so the cat continues to point into the wind), and help the MOB back aboard.

1 Crew overboard!

2 Release the jibsheet and sail away on a reach

3 Bear away

4 Gybe around

5 Return on a close reach

6 Controlling your speed as you appraoch

7 Slowing down and heading up so the crew is alongside the windward hull

8 And they can climb back on board

When approaching the victim in extreme conditions it is often better to stop the catamaran with the person between the hulls by the main beam. This secures their position and allows you to retrieve them over the rear beam as in a capsize. It also prevents the bow, which has a large windage area, blowing away from the victim as you make your final approach.

Man overboard for single-handed sailors is a problem! If the situation occurs, you are best to release hold of the tiller extension but hold onto the mainsheet, causing your mainsail either to sheet in and cause a capsize or to stall and the catamaran to stop. Either way it is your best chance for getting yourself back on board without outside support.

1 Steer carefully and stop with the crew between the hulls

2 The crew can then move under the trampoline

3 To the back of the cat

4 And then be helped on board

MAN OVERBOARD TROUBLESHOOTING

Problem	Cause	Solution
The catamaran is too powerful to manage easily single handed	Not releasing the jib	Let the jib flap as you do the manoeuvre
Trying to tack round and failing	In strong winds, with the jib flapping, you are unlikely to achieve a successful tack	Gybe round instead
You cannot return to the MOB on a close reach	Not going far enough away to gybe	Circle round again, gybing further away
You arrive too fast, or out of position so you cannot pick up the MOB to windward	Not coming back to the MOB on a close reach	Circle round again and slow down as you sail towards the MOB by letting the sail out
You lose steerage at the critical moment and drift off	Insufficient boatspeed on the final approach to the MOB	Take care to keep some speed to maintain steerage until you have reached the MOB

All small catamarans are liable to capsize and, unless you want a sophisticated machine and have a great deal of experience, the catamaran you choose must be easily righted after a capsize.

There are two final situations with a capsize: either the catamaran will lie on its side (90° capsize) or it will invert (180° capsize, or 'turning turtle'). Most modern catamarans have positive mast buoyancy to aid them to lie on their sides in the water, but a full inversion is always a possibility, for a variety of reasons.

90° CAPSIZE & RECOVERY

- Since catamarans float high on their sides, with a large amount of windage, it is important that you keep in contact with your catamaran as it capsizes by holding on to the mainsheet or jibsheet, or it may blow away from you. The catamaran is your liferaft, so hang on!
- Lower yourself into the water, preferably between the foot of the mainsail and the trampoline. Make sure that you do not try to hold yourself out of the water, or you may pull the cat over on top of you.
- Keep in contact with the cat, swim towards the bow and slide your upper body onto the lower hull, forward of the main beam.
- Effectively submerge the bow as a sea anchor and paddle with your feet. This will bring the catamaran around until the mast or bow is pointing into the wind depending on the wind strength.
- Prepare the cat for righting by releasing the mainsheet, jibsheet and traveller and position the tiller extension out over the rear beam. This is important; otherwise the catamaran will try to sail away once it has been righted.
- Position yourselves (both helm and crew) by

the main beam and throw the righting line or the end of the mainsail halyard over the top hull. The amount of crew weight required to right the catamaran will depend on the type and size of craft and the wind strength. The stronger the wind, the easier it is to right a catamaran.

- Lean backwards on the line until your body is almost horizontal to the water (the second crewman may need to assist initially to start the righting of the cat). As the mast breaks the surface, the wind under the sails will help the catamaran come upright. You will find that the momentum created by the wind righting the catamaran can easily capsize it onto the other side. To prevent this one of the team should help start the righting procedure and then move to where the lower hull and main beam meet adding their weight to the underside of the beam to stop it lifting out of the water.
- As the catamaran rotates upright, both of you will end up under the catamaran between the hulls, holding onto the main beam. This is a good safe position which will stop the cat capsizing the other way and will keep you in good

contact with the catamaran, which may try to sail off.

- Once the catamaran is righted you may be able to climb aboard in front of the main beam, but if you have capsized a number of times and are feeling tired, make your way one at a time under the trampoline to the stern of the cat between the hulls. Holding the rear beam, push the tiller bar over to force the catamaran into the wind and climb aboard between the rear beam and tiller connecting bar (the hull buoyancy is low here and it is much easier to climb aboard).

- Once you are both safely aboard, stow away any loose lines, set the rudders and sails, and sail away – learning from the experience!

1 Prepare the cat by releasing the sheets

2 Stand on the bow to turn the cat so the mast / bow is facing into the wind

3 Taking your weight on the righting line and begin to pull the cat upright

4 As the cat begins to come upright one of you moves down to the lower hull

5 And as it comes upright the bottom one puts their weight on the beam

6 To prevent it capsizing the other way

7 One person acts as anchor at the main beam, the other goes astern under the trampoline

8 He climbs back on board over the stern

9 And the other over the bow, or he could go under the trampoline to the stern

Righting A Single-Handed Cat

1 Prepare the cat by releasing the sheets

2 Throw the righting line…

3 Over the hull

4 Lean back on the righting line

5 And begin to pull the cat upright

6 As it comes upright

7 Go to the lower hull

8 To prevent it capsizing the other way

9 Go under the trampoline and climb back in over the stern

180° CAPSIZE & RECOVERY

A fully inverted capsize will often be caused by keeping your weight on the catamaran when you are capsizing. To avoid this, when you have reached the point of no return, get ready to lower yourself into the water: if you delay too long, your weight may well pull the upper hull right over and turn a simple capsize into a complete inversion.

Nevertheless, a fully inverted capsize is not a problem with modern catamarans which have positive mast buoyancy.

- Once the catamaran is totally inverted, climb onto the underside of the trampoline.
- Make sure the jibsheet, mainsheet and traveller line are released.
- Decide which hull is closest to the wind and position yourself on the downwind hull around the stern area with the righting line coming from the windward hull.
- Lean back to raise the windward hull at the bow and move the mast into a position where it wants to float to the surface.
- As the hull becomes clear of the water at the bow it will quickly allow the mast to float to the surface and you will need to move your weight forward to stop the bow rising too high.
- Once the catamaran is on its side follow the procedure for a 90° capsize.

1 Recover the righting line

2 Feed it around the windward hull

3 Position yourselves near the stern to raise the bows

4 Begin to rotate the cat upright

5 And onto its side

6 From here you follow the procedure for a 90° capsize

OTHER TECHNIQUES

These are standard righting techniques: you may need to modify some points slightly depending on a particular catamaran design.

There are two other circumstances when different techniques may be required:

- In light winds you won't get the help from the wind to lift the sail.
- If you lack the physical weight necessary to right an inverted or capsized catamaran.

Lowering the mainsail can help in light winds as you will only be raising the mast weight, not the sail which creates added weight.

Alternatively, if there is a rescue boat, it can help start the righting sequence by lifting the mast or raising the shroud from the windward side. But, if you don't have that help, there are two more options:

RIGHTING BAG

This is a bag which you can fill with water and place on your chest to increase leverage.

HARNESS HOPPING

This can be done if there are two of you and at least one is wearing a trapeze harness.

Using this technique, there is very little weight on the trapezing person as this is taken through the harness spreader bar, but a little natural balance and confidence is an advantage!

1 Position the righting line over the hull: one person (usually the lighter) hooks the righting line to their trapeze harness and the other person steps on

2 Move the weight out to give additional leverage

1 Fill the righting bag with water

2 Seal the bag

3 Put it on your body

4 Straighten your legs to provide additional leverage

CAPSIZING TROUBLESHOOTING

Problem	Cause	Solution
You lose contact with the catamaran, which rapidly drifts away	Not holding onto a line as the cat goes over	Make sure you hold onto a line when you capsize
Falling into the sail (avoid this if at all possible: you may break battens, damage the sail and/or lose contact with the catamaran)	Not getting ready to drop into the water as you capsize	Drop into the water as soon as you pass the point of no return
Inverting fully	Not getting ready to drop into the water as you capsize	Don't leave your weight on the cat as you capsize but drop into the water
Difficulty in starting the righting procedure	Not enough combined crew weight as leverage	Consider using a dry bag filled with water, or harness hopping technique
The catamaran is very difficult to right	Not turning the cat so the mast / bow points towards the wind	Submerge the bow using body weight and use your legs to paddle the bow towards the wind
The catamaran rises and capsizes again onto the other hull	Not releasing all the control lines	Make sure you release the control lines before you start righting the cat
	Weight is not transferred to the lower hull as the cat rotates upright	Ensure crew weight is transferred to the lower hull area as the hull rotates upright
The catamaran starts to sail away when righted	Not releasing all the control lines before righting and / or traveller car obstructed	Make sure you release the control lines before you start to right the cat and place tiller extension over the stern

You have had a good sail and are now on your way back to the beach. Think ahead before landing since a great deal of damage can result if you don't take care. Always check that the area is clear of obstacles and other craft where possible.

As with launching (p52-55), the way you land will depend on the direction of the wind.

The following descriptions are for a two-man catamaran. A single-handed sailor does the same, just on their own.

LANDING WITH THE WIND

ALONG THE SHORE

This is the easiest wind direction for landing.

Choose a cross-wind landing so the catamaran arrives on a reach in an area clear of obstacles and other craft.

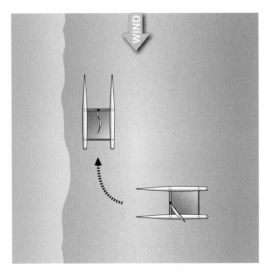

Landing with the wind along the shore

- A safe distance from the beach – about 20 boat lengths – the crew releases the jib and raises the leeward board (if fitted).
- At the same time, ease the mainsheet to slow the catamaran down, until it is moving slowly.
- As helm, cross to the leeward side and lift the leeward rudder (alternatively ask the crew), so it is just in the water.
- Return to the windward side and slowly sail the catamaran towards the beach using the mainsail only as an accelerator and steering from the tiller connecting bar.
- As you reach the beach, head the cat gently into the wind, lifting the windward rudder and

board (if fitted) and easing all the mainsheet and traveller line.

- The crew enters the water from the windward hull, in front of the shroud, making their way to the bow and bridle wire to hold the catamaran head to wind. This is a safe and controlled way for the crew to ensure that they maintain control when the catamaran stops.
- With the catamaran in a safe position, the crew holds the bow and bridle wire while the helm releases the mainsail downhaul, detaches the mainsheet, locks the rudders in the raised position, and prepares the cat for recovery.

1 Release the jib and mainsail to slow the cat

2 Raise the leeward rudder

3 Head up into the wind as the crew prepares to get off, lifting the windward rudder

4 The crew gets off and moves to the bow to hold the cat head to wind

LANDING WITH AN OFFSHORE WIND

When you are sailing back to a windward shore you will often find the wind very gusty and variable in direction. This is because the air is blowing over the land, around trees, hills and houses. If the landing area is restricted you will need to return to the beach on a beat with your sails sheeted right in.

Choose the tack that will give you the most favourable angle back to the beach (A in the diagram) and raise your leeward rudder and board (if fitted) as you get close. Keep your catamaran moving forward or you will lose steerage and the cat will either turn into the wind and stop or go on a reach and gather speed.

Release the jib as you approach the shore and use the mainsheet to control your boatspeed. As you get into shallow water, point the catamaran into the wind and lift the windward rudder and board (if fitted). The crew slides over the side in from the normal place (windward side of the windward hull) once shallow enough and moves to the bow and bridle wire.

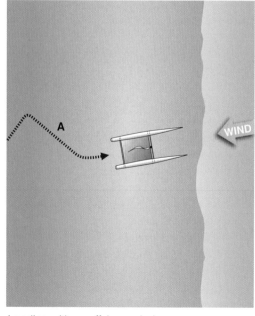

Landing with an offshore wind

LANDING WITH AN ONSHORE WIND

Landing with an onshore breeze needs careful planning due to the wind and waves trying to run you up onto the beach.

In all but the lightest winds, the safest option, in a catamaran with a jib, is to return to the shore under jib alone, as you would in a dinghy. If single handed, without a jib, carry out the same procedure, exposing a small area of the mainsail. Before you begin, allow for any tidal drift as the jib will only allow you to sail downwind.

The first thing to master is the art of lowering the mainsail at sea (which may differ according to your halyard lock, but the following explains a common one):

- Start on port tack and heave-to by backing the jib.
- Release the mainsail downhaul and prepare the halyard to run.
- Pull up on the main halyard: if you are on port tack, with the sails blowing over to the star-

board side, by turning the mast to port the halyard lock will automatically disengage.

- Once the sail is released from the halyard lock, roll the sail as it is lowered leaving the main halyard still attached (so that you don't lose the sail overboard).
- Store the mainsail under the toe straps to prevent the wind taking control of it.

Turn the catamaran downwind and sail under jib alone towards the beach.

Just before you land, lift the rudders (and boards, if fitted) and release the jibsheet. The crew should be ready to slide over the side, in the normal fashion, and turn the cat back into the wind.

An alternative option, particularly for those without a jib, sometimes available to you is to head the catamaran into wind just off the shoreline and prepare the cat as you would for leaving a windward shore allowing the cat to drift backwards towards the beach.

1 Heave to on port tack and release the mainsail downhaul and spanner line

2 Prepare the halyard to run

3 Pull the main halyard, rotate the mast and the halyard lock will release

4 Lower the main, rolling it as you go

5 Leave the halyard attached and store the main

6 Sail downwind to the shore under just the jib

LANDING WITH AN ONSHORE WIND IN SURF

The most efficient way of returning to a lee shore in surf is to sail in line with the wave pattern straight up the beach. This may sound a little extreme and you need some knowledge of the ground ahead, but the options of turning into the wind or coming in under jib alone, could lead to far worse problems.

Prepare the catamaran early, outside the surf break line. Release the mainsail downhaul to de-power the sail. Move all crew weight to the back of the cat and choose an area to land on.

Turn the catamaran downwind and on a line with the surf. Keep sailing at a speed that gives you good steerage. Raise the boards (if fitted). As you approach the beach, the rudders should be triggered last thing, steering all the time. When your catamaran slides onto the beach ease the sails, carefully turn the cat into the wind, as quickly as possible, as there will be considerable pressure on the sails.

LOWERING THE SAILS

You can lower the sail while on the water, or on the beach, but only if you keep the catamaran pointing into the wind.

Lower or furl the jib first, to prevent damage from uncontrolled flapping. How you do this will depend on the locking system on your cat. For the one

shown in the photos, release the jib downhaul line and unhook the jib halyard lock by alternately pulling the jib up by the halyard and down at the tack (bottom front corner). Lower the sail and carefully store it temporarily on the trampoline. Other cats may have a different lock system.

1 Release the jib downhaul line

2 Pull the head up with the halyard while pulling down on the tack

3 This will release the hook

4 Allowing you to lower the sail

To lower the mainsail on most modern catamarans position the catamaran head to wind pull up on the main halyard to raise the halyard lock ring. While keeping the halyard tensioned turn the mast to port, which swings the mast hook away from the lock ring and releases the sail. Finally, release the tension on the halyard and lower and roll the sail.

As discussed previously, there are various forms of masthead and jib halyard lock systems, but the basic principles are the same as described.

Make sure you de-tension the battens before rolling the sail and stowing it away permanently. For safety never leave your catamaran unattended with the sails hoisted.

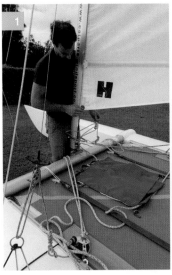

1 Release the mainsail downhaul

2 Remove the sail from the groove

3 Pull the halyard to raise the lock ring, then rotate the mast to port

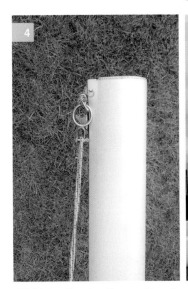

4 Which will swing the masthead hook away from the locking ring

5 And allow you to lower the sail

6 Which you roll up while lowering it

Initially boat tuning is not as important as learning key boat-handling skills. It is only when you are looking for that marginal percentage of extra boatspeed that you need to start looking at tweaking / tuning the adjustments on your catamaran. Whilst systems may vary, the principles of tuning and the effect it has stay the same.

Tuning involves making adjustments to the catamaran, within class rules, to increase its speed. Depending on the class this can range from expensive modifications, such as buying different sails and replacing substantial gear, to small alterations to the mast rake and sheeting angle, which are 'built into the boat' and cost nothing.

STRICT ONE-DESIGNS

Strict one-design catamarans are those which must be sailed as supplied by the builder. Usually all the normal tuning adjustments such as mast rake and sheeting angle are permitted, but the rules do not allow individual interpretation or expensive new equipment. This ensures good class racing at minimum cost and usually supports good second-hand boat values, product and technical support.

Examples of strict one-designs are the Dart 18, Sprint 15, Hobie 16 and Flying Phantom.

RESTRICTED ONE-DESIGN

Restricted classes have rules that are fairly flexible and allow a personal choice in quite a few aspects of the catamaran, layout of control lines, use of blocks and systems etc.

Examples of restricted one-designs are the Nacra 17, Tornado, Hurricane, Spitfire, Viper and SL16.

Nacra 17: A restricted one-design

OPEN CLASS / BOX RULE

These classes have very large tolerances in all areas, allowing considerable scope for different hull and sail shapes. The craft in these classes are for the enthusiast who wants to experiment and has ideas they want to put into practice. The catamarans quickly become out-of-date and therefore the second-hand values are normally low.

Examples of open classes are the A Class and C Class; examples of box rule classes are the F18 and F16.

BASIC TUNING CONTROLS

The principal adjustments that can be made to almost all catamarans (including strict one-designs) are as follows:

- Mast controls:
  - » Mast rake
  - » Shroud tension
  - » Mast rotation
- Jib controls
  - » Jib fairlead position
  - » Jib luff tension
- Mainsail controls
  - » Batten tension
  - » Mainsail luff tension
  - » Mainsheet tension & traveller

In some classes, other adjustments (if fitted) may be made:

- Rudder rake
- Rudder toe in / out
- Board angle

To understand the effect of the sail controls, it is a good idea to turn your catamaran on its side on the beach, support the mast and experiment with the various tensions (as shown in some of these photos). Observe the changes in sail shape: adding more luff and sheet tension flattens the sails, while more batten tension hardens the leech.

MAST CONTROLS

Mast Rake

The rake of the mast is the amount by which it leans forward or backwards from the upright position. Forward rake gives the catamaran leeward helm; that is, by moving the centre of effort forward the cat will try to turn away from the wind, which is not something any discerning sailor wants! By leaning the mast back, the centre of effort moves back and the catamaran will want to turn up towards the wind.

The rake on the mast also affects the trim of the catamaran, pushing it down at the bow when it is raked forward and down at the stern when raked back.

Ideally, rake the mast so there is a gentle pull on the tiller extension when you are beating, with the catamaran trimmed correctly though crew positioning.

Shroud Tension

A firm rig, which does not allow the mast to move (except to rotate), will ensure that you get maximum power from the sails. A loose rig which allows the mast to lean sideways is one way of depowering the rig in strong winds. A disadvantage of a loose rig is that the mast and sails bounce around in light winds or choppy sea conditions, resulting in loss of power and preventing the sails from setting.

Mast Rotation

On 'production one-design' classes, without diamonds, the mast rotation is largely fixed by a control line or a mast stop to provide the best airflow across a wide range of conditions with no fine adjustment.

The mast rotation control limits the mast rotation: the tighter the adjustment the less the mast rotates. If the class rules allow, adjust the control line so the mast lines up with the leeward side of the mainsail, initially pointing towards the leeward shroud. This normally works best with diamond wire supported masts.

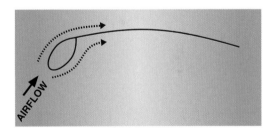

Correct mast rotation: smooth airflow across mast and sail

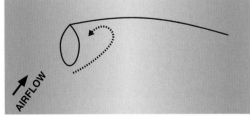

Too much mast rotation: disturbed airflow across mast and sail

JIB CONTROLS

Jib Fairlead Position

The position of the jib fairlead contributes to the shape of the jib and affects the tension on the jib's leech and foot. If the fairlead is moved forward it attracts a tighter leech for a given jib sheet tension, effecting the slot between the jib and mainsail. While a reduced slot can accelerate airflow, when too narrow the airflow may stall in the slot. A narrower slot between the jib and mainsail works better in light to medium winds.

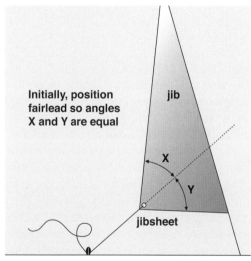

Initially, position fairlead so angles X and Y are equal

jib

X

Y

jibsheet

Jibsheet angle

With the fairlead moved aft the jib leech has less tension and the foot more for a given sheet tension, allowing the leech to open easily when the jib sheet is slightly eased. This is useful in strong winds to allow excessive airflow to pass quickly through the slot. As a starting point, position the fairlead as shown in the diagram. On some catamarans the sheeting angle is adjusted on the clew plate and the slot adjustment by moving a point on the main beam.

Note: In strong winds a narrow slow with significant airflow trying to pass through it can contribute to a mast inverting (bending the wrong way) and can cause terminal damage to the mast or even mast failure.

Jib Luff Tension

The luff tension on the jib is crucial to the catamaran's pointing ability because it controls the shape of the forward part of the sail. Some cats have wire in the luff so the tension is set, others have a soft luff, allowing the luff tension to be altered.

In light winds you will need minimal luff tension to maintain reasonable fullness in the jib approximately one-third of the way aft but, as the wind increases, this fullness gets blown backwards towards the leech unless the luff tension is increased.

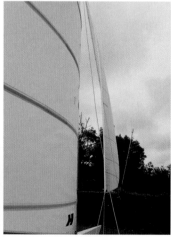

Narrow, uneven slot. Too closed   *Even slot. Good airflow*   *Open, uneven slot. Reduced power. (However may be required for strong winds)*

To set the tension on land, pull on mainsheet tension to tension the forestay as you plan to have it when sailing. Now sheet in the jib on one side so the sail backwinds. Tighten the jib downhaul until the luff is almost as tight as the forestay, you will see the sail shape change as you increase tension. Once you have the luff shape you desire tie or cleat off. (NB. Take care, when the jib or mainsail is cleated, to avoid an onshore capsize!)

To set up the jib luff tension, first tighten the mainsheet to give a straight mainsail leech which tightens the forestay, you can then tighten the jib luff until the tension almost matches that of the forestay

MAINSAIL CONTROLS
Batten Tension

A catamaran sail is curved in cross-section like a bird's wing. The firmness of the curve or camber can be increased and decreased by altering the batten tension. This, along with downhaul, mast rotation / diamonds etc (if fitted), control the power produced.

The more tension in the battens the more the sail will hold its shape and support the leech and the better it is suited to moderate winds. With less tension, the sail is easier to flatten and better suited to strong winds where too much power can be generated or light winds where too much canver can prevent the airflow from passing across the sail.

Whatever your decision on the day, make sure that the tension is even on all battens, giving an even camber along the mainsail. In extreme conditions the top few battens can be slackened off more

than the lower ones to induce flatness in the top of the mainsail or, in some catamaran classes, stiffer battens can be used.

Mainsail Luff Tension

The mainsail downhaul controls the luff tension and hence the fullness of the mainsail. This is done by bending the mast to the shape of the sail luff. Enough tension is needed first, to give the sail shape, but thereafter the amount depends on the wind strength: the stronger the wind, the more the fullness of sail gets blown back towards the leech. So, in strong winds, tighten the luff to keep the maximum curve in the most efficient position – one-third of the way aft (from luff to leech). The effect of adding downhaul tension is to bend the mast and remove depth in the sail as well as opening the leech.

With the main downhaul slack, there is little camber in the sail and very little power is generated: the cat is effectively 'out of gear'

Tightening the downhaul puts camber and power into the sail

Mainsheet Tension & Traveller

If the mainsheet tension is excessive it can hook the leech on the beat

The correct sheet tension gives a smoother, more efficient profile

If the mainsheet tension is too loose it gives excessive twist and you lose power

By dropping the traveller and leaving the sheet as it is, you retain the efficient sail shape in strong winds

If you keep the traveller in the centre on the reach, but slacken the mainsheet, you will get excessive twist in the mainsail shape and find the cat difficult to control

TUNING TABLE

	LIGHT WINDS	MEDIUM WINDS	STRONG WINDS
Jib fairlead position	Equal sheeting angle between leech and foot	Equal sheeting angle between leech and foot so jib telltales break at same time	Sheeting angle moved aft so the jib leech opens before the foot and the upper jib telltale breaks before the lower
Jib luff tension	Light tension	Medium tension	Firm tension – almost as tight as forestay
Batten tension	Light tension – to limit sail camber and allow air to flow easily over the sail surface	Firm tension – to give maximum camber and power	Reduce tension in top battens to flatten the sail and depower the top of the rig and reduce heeling
Mainsail luff tension (downhaul)	Just enough tension to shape the mainsail	Enough tension to give the sail a good curve and prevent creases from the battens when the mainsheet is pulled in	Maximum tension to bend the mast and contribute to flattening the mainsail
Mainsheet tension (upwind)	Sufficient sheet tension to close the leech without hooking it		
Traveller (upwind)	Centre of rear beam	Centre of rear beam or slightly offset, depending on total crew weight and pointing angle	10–50% down to allow mainsail to be sheeted in to maintain limited camber allowing air to flow quickly across sail

Having made sure that the catamaran and your boat handling are up to scratch, then racing is available to you! The following pages will give you a basic knowledge of racing, the Racing Rules, and enough advice on tactics and strategy to help you stay with the pack. Other more specific racing books are available, notably Fernhurst Books' *Sail to Win* series.

Courses will vary at individual clubs but the standard courses used at most championships and open meetings consist of a series of 'triangle' and / or 'sausage' legs with a set number of rounds.

In catamaran specific races the wing mark (if set) is usually angled to allow a close reach followed by a broad reach, rather than two broad reaches.

THE RULES

A full discussion of the rules is outside the scope of this book (refer to Bryan Willis' *Rules in Practice* or *Racing Rules Companion*). For the cautious beginner, a few key rules will keep you out of trouble in most cases.

BOATS MEETING ON OPPOSITE TACKS

A boat is either on a port tack or a starboard tack. It is on a port tack if the wind is blowing over its port side and the sail is on the starboard side.

In the diagram, A, B, and C are on port tack; D, E and F are on starboard tack.

A port tack boat must keep clear of a starboard tack boat.

D, E and F have right of way over A, B and C, who must keep clear: either going behind the starboard boat or tacking onto starboard, whilst keeping clear of the starboard boats.

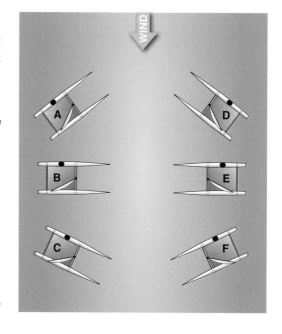

Boats on port and starboard

BOATS MEETING ON THE SAME TACK

If the boats are **overlapped** (if the bow of the following boat is ahead of an imaginary line at right angles to the stern of the leading boat), then:

A windward boat shall keep clear of a leeward boat.

So G must keep clear of H, I must keep clear of J and L must keep clear of K.

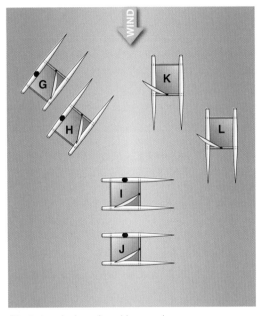

Boats to windward and leeward

If the boats are **not overlapped**:

A boat clear astern shall keep clear of a boat clear ahead.

If M is sailing faster, he is not allowed to sail into the back of N.

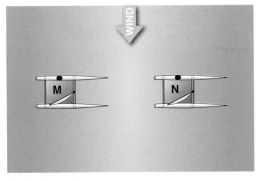

Boat clear astern

BOATS MEETING AT MARKS

When two or more boats approach a mark, the outside boat must give room to the overlapped boat on the inside. This overlap must exist when the leading boat enters the imaginary three boat length circle around the mark.

In the diagram, Boat A has an inside overlap on boat B when they reach the three boat length circle around the mark. This means that B must give room for A to round the mark.

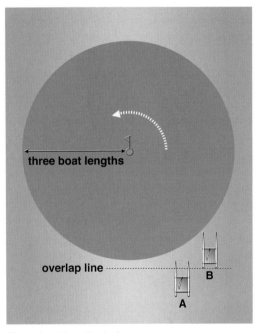

Three boat length circle

However, this rule does not apply on two occasions. It does not apply:

- At the start marks when approaching the line to start. At this time, an inside overlap does not give you right to room.
- When boats are beating towards a mark on opposite tacks: in this case, port gives way to starboard as normal.

For boats on a run, about to round the leeward mark, port and starboard effectively switches off at the 3 boat length distance: the outside boat must give the inside boat room (irrespective of what tack they are on) to round and, if necessary, to gybe.

PENALTIES

We all make mistakes! If you tangle with another boat, decide whether or not you were in the right. If you consider it was your mistake you must either immediately sail clear of other boats and carry out a 360° turn, including 1 tack and 1 gybe, or retire from the race. (The Racing Rules, as standard, require a 720° turn, but for catamarans it is usually reduced to a 360° turn at catamaran events. If you are sailing against other types of craft – dinghies, keelboats, etc. – the standard 720° penalty turn would normally apply. If the standard 720° penalty does not apply, it will be confirmed in the event sailing instructions.)

If you feel the other boat is at fault, but the other team disagree with you, you may launch a protest by hailing "Protest" immediately. There will be information in the event's sailing instructions on how to proceed from there.

The Protest Hearing will be held after the race to hear each boat's story and decide who was in the right.

If you hit a mark of the course when rounding it, you also have to take a penalty: this time a 360° turn for all craft no matter how many hulls you have!

THE START

The start is a very important part of the race. If you get a bad start, you have to overtake everyone to win and, while you're battling past the opposition, the leaders are sailing further ahead. If you get a good start, you're sailing in clear air and the leading pack.

HOW IS A RACE STARTED?

Most races are started on a beat. The race committee sets an (imaginary) start line, usually between the masts of the committee boat (A) and a buoy (B). They often lay another buoy (C), which does not have to be on the line, but boats are not allowed to sail between C and A.

Typically, the starting sequence is as follows (although some clubs may vary):

- 5 minutes before the start: the class flag is raised on the committee boat and a sound signal made.
- 4 minutes before the start: the Blue Peter (code flag P) is raised and a sound signal made.
- 1 minute before the start: the Blue Peter is lowered and a sound signal made.
- At the start: the class flag is lowered and a sound signal made.

(NB. The flag is the signal; the sound is for indication only. There are a number of other flags related to starting and information you may need, so buy a race flag sticker to refer too and place it on your boat.)

Boats must be behind the start line at the start: your aim is to be just behind the line, sailing at full speed, when the race starts.

HOW CAN I GET A GOOD START?

Set your stopwatch at the 5 minute signal and check it at the 4 minute flag signal, along with any other race flags hoisted.

During the last few minutes, avoid the 'danger' areas of X and Y. From area X you cannot get on the start line because the boats to leeward have right of way. Boat D, for example, will be forced the wrong side of buoy C. In area Y you are bound to pass the wrong side of buoy B. Boat F has this problem.

Your catamaran will 'sit' quietly on starboard without moving forward too much, but will drift sideways steadily. Decide where you want to start and, with about 1-2 minutes to go, position yourself several lengths to the right of the spot where you want to be at the start signal, on starboard, with your sails flapping. If necessary, back the jib to prevent turning into the wind. Try to 'hang' in the same position, using the sails to control your boatspeed, and try to be a few boat lengths behind the start line 10-15 seconds before the start.

In the last 10-15 seconds bring the boat up to full speed to cross the line immediately after the start signal.

All this is easier said than done, as all the other boats will be attempting to do the same thing. In particular, watch out for leeward boats who are allowed to luff boats to windward: luff early yourself to maintain a gap between both boats. G must keep clear of I but may luff H.

Single-handed catamarans, without a jib, are liable to round up into the wind just when you want to put your foot down. Practice going from stationary to maximum speed, noting the angle your cat needs to be positioned in relation to the wind and current at the time. How you bring your cat up to speed will vary from catamaran to catamaran, so understanding how your cat reacts is critical for a good start.

Don't reach down the line with 15 seconds to go like boat J. You will have no rights over G, H and I, who are to leeward and will sail into you.

Any boat starting on port (K) must give way to the starboard tack boats.

When you become more experienced you may try starting on port yourself, as it saves one tack later on and could take you to the favoured side of the course. However, it is not recommended for the beginner.

STARTING TECHNIQUE

1 Decide on your starting position
2 Listen for the 5 minute signal and start your stopwatch
3 Practise crossing the line from a stationary position, 'the wind-up'
4 Check your watch at the 4 minute signal & check flags
5 Keep clear of luffing boats to leeward and note the 1 minute signal
6 Increase your speed just before the start signal
7 Go for speed after the start and hold a clear lane

PART 2

111

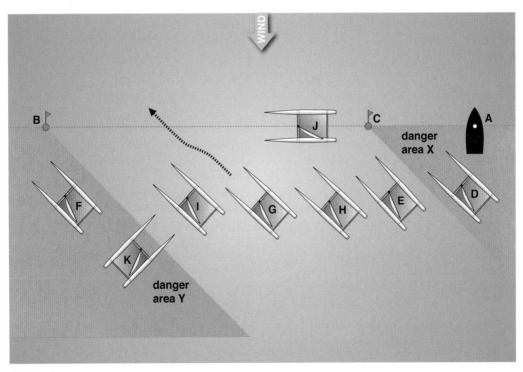

Starting line

THE BEAT

After the excitement of the start, it's important to settle down and concentrate on sailing hard and fast, looking for every advantage to break clear.

WHAT ABOUT OTHER BOATS?

Other boats have an effect on the wind:

- There will be a wind shadow downwind of them.
- There is also an area of disturbed air to windward owing to the wind being deflected by the sail.
- The air behind the boat is also badly disturbed.

You should therefore avoid sailing in another boat's wind shadow, just to windward of it or behind it. In the diagram:

- B should either tack or bear away to clear its wind.
- D and F should both tack, but should LOOK for other boats before they do!

WHICH WAY SHOULD I GO?

You may have to modify your course to take account of tides and windshifts, but your first aim should be to make reasonably long tacks to start with, shortening them as you approach the windward mark. A good basic plan is:

- Start on starboard sail two third of the way up the beat.
- Tack onto port and sail towards the windward mark lay line.
- When just beyond the layline, tack onto starboard into a clear lane as you approach the mark.

Generally look to sail inside the laylines (the path you would sail when beating to arrive at the windward mark). Sailing out to the laylines exposes you to potential changes in wind direction or pressure which you will find harder to capitalise on if you are already on the lay line.

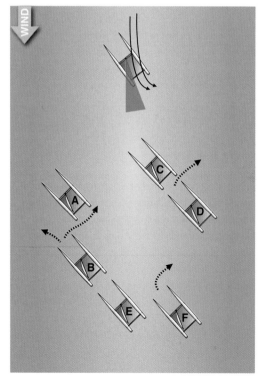

Effect of wind shadow

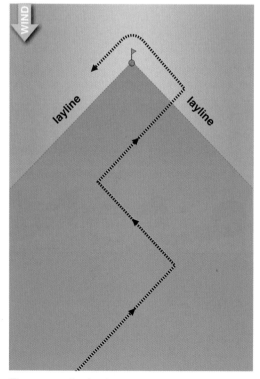

The way up the beat

Don't sail into the area beyond the lay lines – if you do, you will have to bear away and reach into the buoy and will lose valuable time and distance.

For safety's sake arrange your tacks so that you come into the mark on starboard tack. This gives you right of way over boats approaching on port tack, and this could be very useful when you meet at the mark.

WINDSHIFTS

Once you are confident at beating and can tack efficiently, you are ready to start using windshifts.

The wind constantly alters in direction about its mean. Some of the shifts are more pronounced and last longer than others – it is these that you have to spot and use.

In shifty winds, don't go too far from the middle of the beat. Tack if the wind heads you (forces you to alter course away from the mark). In the left-hand diagram the cat takes no account of windshifts. Note how little progress it makes compared with the cat in the right-hand diagram which tacks on each major windshift. On a beat of 200 metres, with

a 9 degree windshift at the start, and another half way up the beat: a cat that tacked correctly on both windshifts will be 100 metres ahead of a cat that tacked wrongly on them!

The main problem is to differentiate between a real shift and a short-lived change in the wind direction. For that reason, sail into each shift for a short period or alternatively look at the angle of the cats sailing ahead.

If you find yourself tacking too often, or if you get confused, sail on one tack for a while until you are sure what the wind is doing. Remember that you lose boat lengths each time you tack a catamaran, so there has to be good reason to do so.

SUBSEQUENT BEATS

As you near the top of the beat, try to see which side of the beat paid off – how did the leaders sail up the beat? Capitalise on this on the next beat by choosing the best route. It should also be easier to choose where you want to go because the fleet will have spread out a bit more.

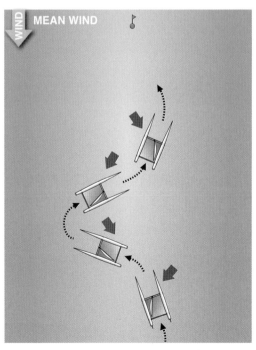
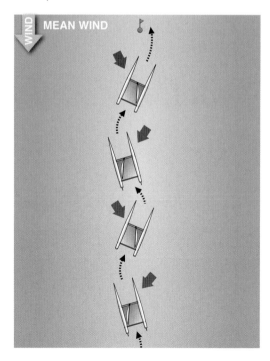

Not tacking and tacking on the windshifts

THE REACHES

THE CLOSE REACH

The quickest way across the reach is a straight line from one mark to the next. However, if your rivals allow you to sail this course, you're lucky! The problem is that overtaking cat (A) pushes up to windward. The cat to leeward (B) gets nervous about their wind being stolen and steers high to protect themselves. The result is that everyone sails an enormous arc (X) and arrives at the wing / spreader mark high and needs to drop back down, causing them to lose ground on the leaders.

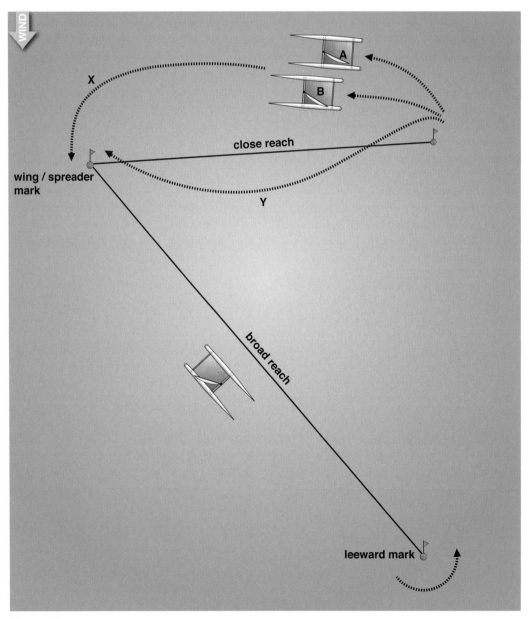

The reach

You have to decide whether or not to go on the 'great circle'; the alternative is to sail a leeward course (Y). You have to go down far enough to avoid the blanketing effect of the cats to windward – but usually you will sail a shorter distance than those doing the arc. You will also get the inside turn at the gybe mark. You can go for the leeward route on the next leg of the course too, but this time you may well be on the outside at the next mark rounding.

Overtaking On The Reach

Although it is possible to overtake to leeward, you must drop well downwind to avoid your rival's wind shadow. Usually it is better to pass to windward, keeping a good boat length clear so that they cannot block you by luffing.

If they do luff, you must respond to avoid a collision (you will be to windward). They can continue to luff until you are clear ahead, but they must give you the opportunity and time to respond.

If you are the person who is being overtaken, you must decide whether it is better to protect your position by luffing or allow the faster boat through and not waste time.

ROUNDING THE WING / SPREADER MARK

As you approach the wing / spreader mark try to make sure that no one has an inside overlap on you as you enter the three boat length circle. Set your traveller and initiate the gybe, starting wide of the mark and finishing close. If someone does have an inside overlap you must give them sufficient room to affect their own gybe.

THE BROAD REACH

This is similar to the close reach, but sail it with the traveller further out. Be careful not to go too far upwind in protecting your wind from those behind because you will then be forced to gybe or approach the next mark on a run.

ROUNDING A PORT-HAND LEEWARD MARK

As you approach a leeward mark, as at the wing mark, try to prevent anyone obtaining an inside overlap as you enter the three boat length circle. Take the mark wide, but come in close as you sheet in to start the beat. Adjust the controls fluently: traveller first (you may ask your crew to pull this in for you), followed by mainsheet and jibsheet together as you steer the catamaran up towards the wind. Make sure you do not stall by sailing too close to the wind: this will make the jib back and the cat will lose speed.

Just as before, try to approach the windward mark on starboard. This time you are going to turn and go downwind to the leeward mark: so ease the jib, mainsheet and traveller, and bear away until the bridle wire wind indicator is at approximately 90° to the cat.

THE DOWNWIND LEG

Decide on your zigzag course downwind, taking into account any extra gusts of wind that you can see on the water. Other boats will also be 'tacking' downwind, so remember the port and starboard rule. Also remember to ensure that you are sailing in clear wind and that boats are not blanketing you.

Gusts of wind travelling down the course are your best opportunity for extra speed, more apparent wind and lower angles of sailing. By keeping an eye to windward you can detect which gusts are worth gybing back into.

ROUNDING A PORT-HAND LEEWARD MARK

As you approach a port hand leeward mark there will often be several other boats with you. If you arrive at the mark on port remember that initially boats coming in on starboard have right of way and, as your boat reaches the three boat length circle, any boat with an inside overlap on port or starboard has room at the mark. If you arrive close to the mark on starboard, you may have right of way as inside boat but you will also have to gybe and sheet in before you can sail to windward.

LEEWARD MARK GATE

A single leeward mark on a downwind leg is often replaced with a leeward mark gate with two marks for you to sail between. You can round either mark and head to the side of the course that you think is most favourable – opening a variety of opportunities.

The three boat length rule is the same for both marks, so catamarans approaching the left hand gate in the diagram on starboard (A), as they enter the three boat length area, need to be aware that they may have to give mark room to cats arriving on port (B)!

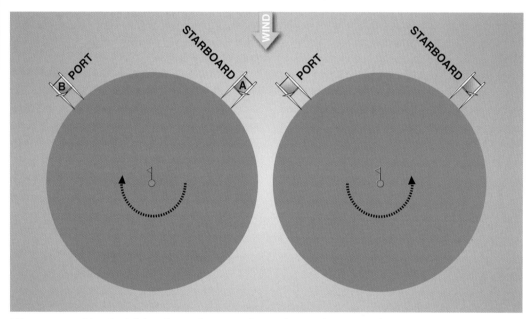

When approaching the left hand gate the port gybe cat has mark room on the starboard cat

THE FINISH

After the correct number of rounds you will be expected to finish! The finish line can be set just to windward of the windward mark or just below the leeward mark / gate and consists of a buoy and a finishing boat. Alternatively it might be between a mark of the course and a finishing boat.

As you sail the final leg, decide whether you can overtake the boat in front. If not, concentrate on covering the boat behind by staying between them and the finish.

After you have crossed the line, congratulate each other and relax. Don't worry if you weren't the first to finish; you weren't the only one. At a later date think about the race and try to analyse your good and not so good decisions so that next time

you are better prepared and one step closer to being race savvy!

In a two-man catamaran this can involve a discussion between you both and you should talk about your options during the race. However, if you are sailing single handed, it is just you in charge of every decision and action that takes place during the race! To make the most of the opportunities that present themselves, you need to learn to sail your catamaran on automatic, while gathering information around you, assessing tactical advantages and observing the positions of your competitors. This is an ability you can only pick up over time: put simply, the more you practice, the better you get!

PART 3

HIGH PERFORMANCE CATS & ADVANCED TECHNIQUES

This part of the book is about getting the most out of a high performance cat, and the chapters cover all points of sailing and rig tuning. However, we all have to start somewhere and so this chapter covers the basics and is for those sailing with a gennaker for the first time.

We would recommend Force 2 for your first attempt sailing with a gennaker:
- Sail upwind to give yourself ample sea room, and check the area you're about to sail into.
- Bear away onto the tack which allows the gennaker to be hoisted on the leeward side (generally starboard tack).
- Set the boards approximately 50% (if fitted).
- Set the mainsail for downwind sailing with the traveller near, if not on, the centre line
- Set the jib as if close reaching.
- Raise the gennaker with the catamaran heading a few degrees below your normal downwind course.
- Once the sail is fully hoisted, bring in the mainsail traveller almost to the centre line. Head up to just above the 45° downwind sailing angle and sheet in the gennaker.
- Lock on to the downwind power, then bear away using the apparent wind created.
- Experiment with the downwind sailing angle, the speed at which the apparent wind is generated, and how the potential sailing angle can change.
- Now experiment with a steady gybe giving the crew time to adjust their position and sheets.
- For your first drop: bear away downwind, recover the gennaker to leeward and stow it. (Starboard tack if fitted with a chute.)

FIRST SAIL: DO'S
- Do check all sharp edges / rings are taped
- Do check all lines and feeds before going afloat
- Do practice the hoist and recovery on land first
- Do keep watch for other craft
- Do communicate with each other during hoisting, recovery and course changes
- Do release the halyard before the tack line when dropping the gennaker

FIRST SAIL: DON'T'S
- Don't raise the gennaker without having sea room
- Don't pass other craft to windward without leaving sufficient space for bearing away
- Don't leave insufficient room to leeward for recovering the sail and preparing for upwind sailing
- Don't release the halyard before the recovery line or clew is under tension, ready to be recovered

HOISTING THE GENNAKER

STRAIGHT HOIST

Hoisting the gennaker to leeward is the fastest and most convenient way to hoist. The sail is immediately positioned on the correct side of the catamaran, which can then be brought up to speed smoothly and efficiently.

- Bear away to just below the normal downwind sailing angle.
- Adjust, as required, other controls for downwind sailing: downhaul, mast rotation, jib-sheets, mainsail outhaul, boards etc.

- Check the area to leeward.
- Hoist the gennaker swiftly: on a two-line system pull the tack line out first before hosting; on a one-line system the hoist and outhaul happen automatically.
- Once fully hoisted, head up to bring the apparent wind indicator approximately 90 degrees across the cat.
- Sheet in the gennaker and mainsheet, power up and alter your course to the induced apparent wind direction.

1 With a two-line system, first pull the tack out

2 When the tack is at the end of the pole, start to hoist the gennaker (with a one-line system) these will happen together)

3 Hoist the gennaker

4 Until it is fully up

5 Then trim the sail

THE GYBE HOIST

In some situations, it can be advantageous to hoist the gennaker as you gybe. For instance, as you round a windward mark and look to head out to the other side of the course area downwind.

- Prepare the boat by setting the daggerboards, downhaul, outhaul, etc. as you bear away.
- Set the tack outhaul line and hoist smoothly while turning the catamaran slowly through a gybe.
- Sheet the gennaker directly on the new lee-ward side.
- Begin to power up the boat once the gennaker is set and crew settled.

TOP TIP

To make life easy for the crew, the helm should turn the boat at such a rate that the gennaker can be fully hoisted before the mainsail changes side.

HOISTING: **DO'S**

- Do check the leeward area before hoisting
- Do pull the outhaul out first before hoisting on a two-line system

HOISTING: **DON'T'S**

- Don't hoist on a reach
- Don't sheet in before the gennaker is fully hoisted

1 With a two-line system, first pull the tack out as you approach the mark upwind

2 As you pass the mark and start to bear away, start hoisting the gennaker (with a one-line system start here)

3 Hoist the gennaker as you bear away

4 So that it is fully up when you prepare to gybe

5 Gybe

6 Then trim the sail on the new side

DROPPING THE GENNAKER

Practising dropping the gennaker can give you a big advantage on the water. It is all a matter of timing. So the more efficient the process is, the faster you are able to be back up to full speed sailing hard on the wind.

STRAIGHT DROP

The advantage of a straight drop is speed. With today's current designs using a chute, a leeward drop is often preferable as it causes least friction and change in course direction.

- Bear away to a low downwind sailing angle to take any load out of the gennaker.
- Tension the chute recovery line before releasing the halyard and tack line.
- Recover the gennaker swiftly: on a two-line system pull the tack line release once the gennaker begins to fill the chute.
- Adjust, as required, other controls for the next direction of sailing: downhaul, mast rotation, jibsheets, mainsail outhaul, boards etc.
- Turn the catamaran into the next sailing direction.

If you are using a bag system: sail downwind, sheet the clew on to the windward side and lower into the bag rather than do a leeward drop behind the mainsail which forces the crew to leeward.

TOP TIP
Remember that while the gennaker is being lowered it is important to keep the cat sailing, adjust the mainsail and jib to adapt to the change in speed now that the gennaker is not filling.

1 Release the gennaker sheet and begin to pull on the retrieval line   *2 Release the halyard*   *3 Pull the gennaker into the chute*

4 Towards the end, release the tack line   *5 So the gennaker is fully in the chute*

TOP TIP
Communication between helm and crew is everything when hoisting, lowering and manoeuvring. Sharing the roles and knowing exactly what the other team member is doing is key.

GYBE DROP

With today's modern race courses, you often encounter a leeward gate mark, this can mean it is necessary to gybe the catamaran while dropping the spinnaker.

- Check area you will be turning into.
- Enter a long slow turning gybe to release pressure in the gennaker.
- Recover the gennaker swiftly before the main sail changes sides.
- Adjust other controls and turn the cat into its new sailing direction.

DROPPING: DO'S

- Do bear away and release the leeward sheet
- Do check the lines are free to run
- Do take the slack out of the recovery line before releasing the halyard

DROPPING: DON'T'S

- Don't lower on a reach
- Don't head up before the gennaker is lowered
- Don't forget to release the outhaul line

PART 3

122

SINGLE HANDED

Sailing single handed with a gennaker is a challenge, but great fun! You only have two pairs of hands and so it is important to work out what you need to continually adjust. One hand has to do the steering, so it is likely that the other will be trimming the gennaker while the mainsheet is cleated off in the optimum position.

Single-handed gennaker hoist and recovery needs time and organisation. You will need to work out what works best for you, but here are some suggestions:

Attach some Velcro material on your tiller extension and at strategic places on the decks so that you can hold the rudders in a straight line, leaving your hands free.

Consider the various pump action gennaker hoist systems that allow one-handed hoists and drops.

Hoist clear of other boats and drop early when approaching a leeward mark rounding so that you have time to position yourself and make adjustments for going upwind.

CAPSIZING

It's advisable not to try to right the catamaran with the gennaker hoisted.

Having capsized: recover the crew, then position yourselves near the bow to act as a sea anchor: turning the cat so that the mast / bow points into the wind (see p91). While one person recovers the gennaker into the chute, the other prepares the catamaran for righting as given on p91. Once righted, re-hoist the gennaker and get back up to speed.

REPAIRING THE GENNAKER

You will inevitably tear the gennaker during use. Typically a gennaker is silicone coated (to help it in and out of the chute) and so patches don't stick very well. You will either have to use a silicone based adhesive or sand it down with wet and dry sandpaper before sticking the patch on. Always carry a repair kit consisting of gennaker repair tape, cleaning fluid and scissors.

To repair the sail:
- Spread it out on a flat surface.
- Clean both sides with methylated spirit (this also eliminates any moisture).
- Cut two patches of repair tape which are larger than the tear and round the corners of the patches.
- Apply them on both sides of the sail.
- Apply even pressure across the whole area with special attention to the edges.
- When possible leave overnight for the glue to cure.

For small nicks, this will probably last for the life of the sail but for major damage you will need to replace it with a proper sailmaker's repair at a later date.

Although sometimes challenging, sailing single handed with a gennaker can be very exciting

HELMING FROM THE WIRE

Sailing a high performance cat, with a big rig, is likely to mean that you will need to double trapeze.

It's important, as helm, that you feel comfortable on the wire and can control the catamaran effectively.

As helm your first objective is to be able to go out on the wire smoothly, whilst in control of the steering and the mainsheet, in a smooth transition. The same is true when you come back into the cat without stalling or changing direction. When you can do all that, you're ready for tacking, gybing etc.

TO GO OUT

Initially there may be a tendency to pull the tiller as you go out on the trapeze which makes your catamaran bear away and pitches you forward, compounding the issue! Begin by sliding your hand out along the tiller extension behind your ear. The mainsheet should be in the other hand so that, when you go out on the trapeze, you will automatically sheet in to create extra power to balance the extra leverage. Now hook on and roll out.

There are two proven ways to get onto the wire, traditionally from a seated position you can shuffle back until you bum drops onto the wire and then step out from there, if you require extra support use you mainsheet hand on the trapeze handle. This technique is shown on p86.

Alternately, to speed the process up, roll onto the wire directly from your knees and sheet the mainsheet as you go, as is shown in the photo sequence here.

1 Start in your normal sailing position, kneeling on the deck

2 Shuffle out, transfer mainsheet to your tiller hand and hook on

3 Return the mainsheet to your front hand and shuffle out

4 Put your front foot on the side

5 And push out

6 Until you are fully extended in your normal trapezing position

TOP TIP

An adjustable trapeze system will make getting on and off the wire far easier, lift your trapeze position so that when rolling out you have less distance to drop before the wire takes the load. This works just as well when getting off the wire.

PART 3

124

HELMING FROM THE WIRE

If it's windy you will need to trapeze low, for maximum leverage and stability, but realistically you will have to be slightly higher than your crew so that you can see where you are sailing. You will be steering with the tiller extension in your back hand and the mainsheet in your front hand, but use the thumb of your tiller hand to hold excess sheet, probably coiled over the thumb.

Trapeze slightly higher than your crew so you can see where you are going

To play the mainsheet you have several options:
- On a long beat, get your crew to secure their jibsheet, then pass the mainsheet for the crew to play. This has proven to be very effective but requires good teamwork.
- For single-handers, or when your crew is busy, simply take two or three turns round your hand, then either pull in or let out as you wish.
- If you want to move large amounts of mainsheet yourself, you'll need to use your tiller hand as a clamp. Preferable do not use the mainsheet jamming cleat as a temporary grip.

Hold the tiller extension in your back hand over your shoulder and the mainsheet in your front hand, but use the thumb of your tiller hand to hold excess mainsheet

COMING BACK IN

The natural tendency is to push the tiller as you come in off the wire, which simply turns the cat into the wind.

Begin by moving your hand down on the shaft of the tiller extension then move in to sit on the side of the boat (as shown on p87) or use the trapeze handle to help you roll over your feet and finish up kneeling on the trampoline and your tiller hand by your ear maintaining a straight line (as shown here).

Tacking from the wire is covered in the next chapter.

1 Transfer the mainsheet to your aft tiller hand

2 Move your tiller extension hand down the tiller

3 Bend your knees

4 Come into a kneeling position and unclip

5 Take back the mainsheet into your front hand

6 Adopt your normal sailing position

We will now go through the techniques of sailing a high performance cat around a course, starting with upwind.

Sailing a high performance cat upwind is all about the compromise between sailing as close to the wind as you can, but not losing too much boatspeed. There are two modes:
- High and slow(er)
- Low and fast

High gets you heading closer to the windward mark, and sailing a shorter distance, but you have to sacrifice some speed. Low means you sail a longer distance, but you travel faster and so can often make up this extra distance. Which you choose will be dependent upon the sea state, wind strength and your crew weight.

Hurricane going upwind

SEA STATE

If the water is flat, with no waves, go high – you can carry your speed a lot better.

If it's choppy or wavy, then you need to keep the power in the catamaran and should go low to drive through the waves.

WIND STRENGTH

In lighter winds, the extra speed through going low isn't that much, so it is usually better to stay high. But if it is light and choppy be careful that the boat doesn't slow too much; sail a little lower to maintain good speed.

As the wind increases to medium strength, the potential for increasing your speed by bearing off a bit is enormous. Let the bow come off the wind a bit and you will accelerate and move up a gear.

When it gets really windy, and you are overpowered, you need to go back towards high mode, feathering the cat into the wind to reduce some of the power.

CREW WEIGHT

With a lighter crew you have less leverage to counteract the power of the wind, so the wind speed you need to start feathering will be lower than for a heavier team who can use the power for longer and are therefore able to sail low and fast in greater wind and fire through the waves.

MEDIUM WINDS

CREW WEIGHT

In a two-man high performance cat, typically both sailors will be on the trapeze in medium winds.

The windward hull should be just flying above the water: being out of the water causes less drag, but you don't want to heel the mast too much because this makes the rig and foils less efficient. Use movement of the crew weight in and out to assist in creating that perfect angle of heel.

AIRFLOW

At the lower end of the wind range, the mast should be rotated sideways giving a fuller entry, moving to facing back, with a flatter entry, when it gets windier. Other mainsail settings would be:

- Downhaul: at the lower end of this wind range, just enough to take the creases out of the sail, but tighter as the wind increases.
- Outhaul: set to give around 50 mm between the boom and the sail on average.
- Traveller: set in the middle of the catamaran.

For the jib your typical settings upwind in medium winds would be:

- Luff tension: Just tight enough to take the wrinkles out of the sail, with no scalloping / creases.
- Jib car position / clewboard and jibsheet tension: Set to ensure that you have a parallel slot between the leech of the jib and the luff of the mainsail.

TECHNIQUE

Sail in low mode: there should be enormous benefits of extra speed in medium wind conditions.

From the wire, the crew would usually play the mainsheet – they have two free hands and are able to adjust the mainsail quickly as required. The helmsman will concern himself with the tiller and the downhaul.

The working range of the mainsheet upwind in medium winds is about a metre, or a crew's arm length. In these wind strengths you are not likely to be very overpowered. At the lower end of the wind range have the mainsail a bit looser, tightening it as the winds get up or in the gusts to give more power.

The daggerboards should be fully down to resist the sideways force.

In medium winds you are both on the trapeze looking to maintain the windward hull just out of the water

LIGHT WINDS

CREW WEIGHT
Your approach should change when it goes light (when only one of the team or neither are trapezing). Now the helmsman should be on board, holding the mainsheet, while the crew is dynamically moving their weight around to provide the correct trim and balance – trapezing if necessary.

Ideally, the windward hull should be just kissing the water, but, in reality, in most light wind conditions it will be in the water.

AIRFLOW
In light winds the mast should be pointing at the shroud base. This gives a smooth transition from mast to sail.

Other mainsail settings would be:
- Downhaul: fully eased, but with enough load to remove horizontal creases from the main.
- Outhaul: set to give around 100 mm between the boom and the sail.
- Traveller: set in the middle of the cat.

The mainsheet should be on tight, but not hard enough to hook the leech to windward. The leech telltales at the top of the mainsail should be streaming 70% of the time. But in these conditions, the mainsheet is quite a dynamic control: as you accelerate in a puff it should be tightened, but as you decelerate it should be loosened to keep the flow over the sail.

For the jib your typical settings upwind in light winds would be:
- Luff tension: Just tight enough to take the

In light winds both hulls will be in the water upwind

wrinkles out of the sail, with no scalloping / creases (as for medium winds).
- Jib car position / clewboard and jibsheet tension: move closer in from medium wind position, but again ensuring that you have a parallel slot between the leech of the jib and the luff of the mainsail.

TECHNIQUE
In light winds you will generally sail in high mode unless there is chop and you need the power to drive through the waves.

The daggerboards should be fully down.

STRONG WINDS

In strong winds, when you are beginning to get overpowered, you need to start depowering the rig. You will both be trapezing again and the mainsheet goes back to the crew with the helm working the tiller and downhaul.

CREW WEIGHT
Lower yourselves on the trapeze so that you are flat with the catamaran, to increase leverage, but, of course, be careful not to get washed off. In big waves, you may need to trapeze higher than the

ideal position. Keep the catamaran as flat as possible with the windward hull flying just above the water.

AIRFLOW

In strong winds the mast rotation should be moving closer to pointing fore and aft. Being closer to fore and aft means that the top of the mast can be blown off to leeward: this helps lose power from the top of the sail and moves the centre of effort down, giving less heeling force.

Other mainsail settings would be:

- Downhaul: hard on: this flattens the sail and helps bend the mast, helping you to keep the mainsheet in tight.
- Outhaul: set so the sail is flat along the boom.
- Traveller: start to ease a bit, which will help you keep the mainsheet fully in.

TOP TIP

Always put the downhaul on before the outhaul. If you do it the other way round you can over tension the foot of the sail and damage the bolt rope.

The mainsheet should be pulled in as tight as possible but, as described above, the other controls can help you minimise the sheeting required. Tight in, the mainsheet acts a bit like a backstay: bending the mast to take the power out of the sail. It therefore becomes a case of using the other controls to minimise easing the mainsheet.

For the jib you now want to flatten it off as much as possible:

- Luff tension: tight.
- Jib car position / clewboard and jibsheet tension: move the car out and have a narrower sheeting angle, meaning that the foot is straight and the leech opens up.

TECHNIQUE

You should start to raise the daggerboards if you are losing forward drive because of the cat heeling.

Gusts & Lulls

In a gust or lull there are a number of ways to depower / power up. Try to identify the most effective option(s) for your situation.

As a gust hits you can:

- Ease the mainsheet to absorb the gust.
- Tighten the downhaul to depower the mainsail.
- Rotate the mast back to narrow the sail entry.
- Ease the jib slightly.
- Raise the daggerboards.
- Ease the traveller.
- Lower yourself on the trapeze.

When the lull comes you can:

- Put the mainsheet back on to put the power back into the rig.
- Raise yourself on the trapeze to reduce leverage and make it easier to move in and out of the catamaran.
- More your body weight in towards the cat and forward – bending the knees and coming off the trapeze.
- Ease the downhaul.
- Ease the rotator away from the fore and aft position to point at the shroud base.

If it gets even lighter:

- Ease the mainsheet to put more depth in the mainsail.
- Ease the jib to mirror what the main is doing.

In strong winds you will need to start to depower

Like any aspect of sailing a high performance cat, tacking requires a bit more concentration and finesse than in a standard cat, even though the basic principles are the same.

MEDIUM & STRONG WINDS

In these conditions, you are both on the trapeze. Communication and observation are key to tacking a high performance cat: check where you are going to turn, that there is room, and count into the tack so you are both ready.

HELMSMAN

- Lift yourself on the trapeze (making it easier to come in).
- Take the mainsheet off the crew and put it in your tiller hand.
- Use your free hand to grab the trapeze handle.
- Pull yourself back on board.
- Allow the tiller hand to ease the catamaran into the wind.
- Get onto your knees on the trampoline.
- Keep the catamaran turning and shuffle your way into the middle of the cat.
- Pass the tiller from one hand to the other around the mainsheet falls – the mainsheet itself remains in the old tiller hand.
- Continue to shuffle over to the new windward side.
- Position yourself on your knees, facing in, with your feet just over the edge of the cat.
- Straighten up the tiller when the tack is completed and the catamaran is at the appropriate angle to the wind.
- The mainsheet will now be in your forward hand, with the tiller in your aft hand and on your aft shoulder.
- Put your mainsheet into your tiller hand and use your now free hand to hook on to the trapeze.
- Take the mainsheet back into your forward hand, taking a wrap of it around your hand (gripping the rope takes a lot of energy and wrapping it around your hand takes the pressure off).
- From your knees, roll out onto the wire, sheeting in the mainsail to maintain heel and give power.
- Once stable, hand the mainsheet back to the crew.
- Lower yourself down on the trapeze into your sailing position.

CREW

- Lift yourself on the trapeze (making it easier to come in).
- Hand the mainsheet to the helm.
- If appropriate, ease the jib slightly to aid acceleration out of the tack when it is complete.
- As the catamaran begins to turn, grab the trapeze handle, pull yourself towards the cat and unhook from the trapeze. (Be aware that the turning of the catamaran will naturally propel

you forwards, so use your legs to absorb any tendency to be thrown forward).

- You shouldn't need to back the jib with daggerboards but, if there is an issue at the back of the cat, holding the jib back at the car can assist the bow round.
- Shuffle across the cat, taking care of the low boom.
- Grab the new trapeze wire (you want to be out on the wire as soon as possible: before the helm).
- Hold the trapeze handle with one hand, moving outboard, and hook on using your free hand.
- As the catamaran accelerates on the new tack, squeeze the jib back on.
- Lower yourself on the trapeze into your sailing position.
- Take the mainsheet of the helm.

1 Get ready to come in from the wire

2 Both come off the wire

3 Turn the cat

4 Start to cross the cat

5 The helmsman swaps hands

6 Get ready on the new tack with the crew clipping on

7 The crew goes out on the wire as the helm clips on

8 Both go out on the wire

9 To their full trapezing position

LIGHT WINDS

In light winds only the crew, or neither of you, will be on the trapeze. You must move smoothly to keep your catamaran going and to encourage air to flow over the sails for as long as possible.

The technique is as described for tacking the standard cat in light winds on p67.

TOP TIP

If you are struggling to pop the top battens on the mainsail through the tack, tighten the down haul until the battens flick over and then loosen it again for optimum sail shape in the lighter winds.

The first part of downwind sailing in a high performance cat is the bear away where you are aiming to turn the catamaran off the wind, hoist the gennaker and get the cat sailing downwind as quickly as possible.

MEDIUM WINDS

Most high performance cats single-wire downwind, although those with foils tend to double trapeze because of the greater power. For this book we will focus on the non-foiling technique.

- As you approach the bear away, helm and crew lift themselves on the trapeze.
- The helm comes into the cat and retrieves the mainsheet.
- The crew stays out on the wire to maintain the sailing angle.
- From the trapeze, the crew pulls the gennaker tack line, pulling the gennaker out to the end of the pole.
- The crew eases the jib (which stops the bow going down).
- The helm pulls the tiller towards them and eases the mainsheet.
- Simultaneously, the crew comes off the trapeze: behind the shroud if it's windy, in front of it if it's light wind.
- Once fully off the wind and stable, the crew hoists the gennaker as quickly as possible.
- As the spinnaker reaches the top, the helm takes the spinnaker sheet and fills the gennaker.
- While the crew pulls the daggerboards up to the downwind position (half way up).
- The crew eases the mast rotator so that it is facing towards the shroud.

- The crew goes on the trapeze as soon as possible, using the helm's trapeze wire to be as far aft as possible, taking the gennaker sheet.
- The helm pulls the mainsheet tighter to stabilise the mast and provide tension against the pull of the gennaker.
- The crew moves back to stop the bow from digging into the waves.
- The helm positions the tiller extension astern and uses the tiller connecting bar to steer.
- The helm finds a solid steering position with their feet under the toestraps.

See photo sequence overleaf.

Bearing Away In Medium Winds

1 Approach the mark the tack is pulled out to the pole

2 The crew comes in off the wire

3 As you round the mark, the crew starts hoisting

4 And hoists as fast as they can

5 Grabbing the gennaker sheet when it is hoisted

6 And clips on ready to go out on the wire

LIGHT WINDS

In light winds you won't need to go as far off the wind as in medium winds to hoist the gennaker. There may also be the opportunity to lift the daggerboards earlier (because the crew will already be down to leeward) and you can therefore get settled on your downwind leg more quickly.

Apart from that, the basic procedure is the same, but without the trapeze steps.

STRONG WINDS

In strong winds, the basic procedure is again the same, but, if it's really windy, you may sacrifice some time to lift the daggerboards before you bear away to make the bear away easier (although you will slow down doing this). During the turn the helm might also ease the traveller to take the weight off the sail, reduce the power and excessive twist in order to stop the bow digging into the waves.

If you are struggling with the bow digging in, you can leave the crew on the trapeze for longer in the rear toe loops, which brings the weight back and makes the boat more stable. But naturally this will delay the hoisting process.

Just as on the beat, with a high performance cat downwind there are two modes. This time:
- Going higher and faster
- Going lower and slower

You are aiming to keep the windward hull just out of the water and this dictates your angle: sail as low as you can, while keeping the hull out of the water.

The fore and aft trim of the catamaran is also very important downwind.

MEDIUM WINDS

CREW WEIGHT

The crew is on the wire, trapezing as far back as appropriate to stop the hull digging in. The helm establishes a stable steering position and steers using the tiller connecting bar.

The aim is to keep the windward hull flying and how this is achieved is described in the 'Technique' section below.

Downwind in medium wind the crew is trapezing at the stern and the helm is in a safe steering position steering with the tiller connecting bar

AIRFLOW

Downwind in medium winds, the crew plays the gennaker from the trapeze, looking to keep the spinnaker on the edge of flapping.

Keep the traveller in the centre. Mast fully rotated and downhaul off.

The jib should be trimmed to keep the telltales streaming relative to the apparent wind.

TECHNIQUE

The steering dictates the height that the windward hull will fly: the closer to the wind you steer, the higher the windward hull will go; the further from the wind, the lower it will fly. The steering needs to be as proactive as possible to minimise rudder movement (which acts as a brake). React to the gusts and lulls as they happen: when the gust hits, bear away; as the lull comes, head up. You are looking for small, smooth movements, anticipating the changes in the wind, rather than heavy dramatic movements which will only slow you down.

A small amount of mainsheet can also be used to help adjust the hull height: ease it slightly when the hull lifts; tighten it when it the hull begins to drop. But steering is far more important than mainsheet adjustment and you certainly shouldn't compromise your steering by trying to adjust the mainsheet.

The boards can be raised to reduce drag and stop the boat becoming overpowered. In turn it allows the boat to move faster forward through the water.

The helmsman and crew must work together to keep the boatspeed up. Initially head up and sheet in a little to make your catamaran accelerate. Then turn away from the wind onto a lower course, easing the gennaker as you turn followed by trimming as the cat accelerates. The catamaran will accelerate further on this new course and the gennaker will need to be re-trimmed to compensate for the apparent wind change. Continue to trim the genna-

ker to changes in wind strength and boat direction. For example, in a gust of wind, the helmsman will bear away and the crew will need to ease the sheet to accommodate this, before sheeting in as the cat accelerates.

The helm may make small adjustments to the mainsheet tension to trim the mainsail to the optimum angle while making small alterations in direction. Much is done by feel but leech telltales are a good indicator to start with of correct mainsheet trim. As medium wind increases there becomes a point where it is possible to dramatically increase speed and direction via the apparent wind by 'hotting up': luffing up to create immediate power and speed which needs instant conversion into downwind sailing by bearing away whilst maintaining the speed and apparent wind.

LIGHT WINDS

CREW WEIGHT

In light winds, if you can fly a hull while still making progress downwind, you should do so. Crew weight can also be used to help fly the hull – moving further to leeward as the breeze decreases.

Once the wind is so light that you cannot fly a hull, then you need to get your weight forward to lift the transom:

- The crew should be on the front beam.
- The helm should be as far forward as they can while still being able to steer with the tiller extension – they need to maintain good control over the rudders.

AIRFLOW

The crew should sit to leeward, controlling the gennaker with gentle and refined movements. Ease the halyard tension to soften the luff of the gennaker and trim the sheet to keep the telltales flowing or the luff just on the curl.

The helm should induce twist into the mainsail by easing the mainsheet while keeping the traveller central.

Rotate the mast across the boat. Depending on the wind strength and distance to sail, ease the

In light winds you have to head up more and still want to try to fly a hull if you can

downhaul to deepen the sail and in turn this loosens the outhaul.

Set the jib to the telltales – normally the close reaching position.

TECHNIQUE

The daggerboards should be between completely down and 50% up. The exact amount you will need to find out by practice: too much raised and the catamaran cannot generate forward power; too much down and the power generated is affected by drag and steering.

The objective is to keep air flowing over the gennaker and power in the sail. This is all about apparent wind: the helmsman steers up and the catamaran accelerates. The helm can then bear away gently, trying to sail low while encouraging the new apparent wind to stay attached. If you go too low, the gennaker collapses or at least the tension in the sheets drops and the speed falls. This is the signal to head back up slightly and repeat the process. But the objective is not to let the gennaker collapse! A good crew communicates to the helm all the time how much pressure there is on the sheet. As soon as the pressure starts to fall the helm can then decide whether they can luff to generate more speed or whether the cause is reduced wind speed or wind shadow from other boats.

STRONG WINDS

CREW WEIGHT

In strong winds it is vital to keep an eye on the leeward bow and ensure that it does not dig into the water. The crew's body weight should be on the wire and as far back as they can go, putting their rear foot into the toe loop on the back corner of the catamaran. The helm should sit on the windward hull, close to the rear beam.

When it gets really windy, you need to move into safety mode: stop trying to fly a hull, so that you have the buoyancy of both hulls to prevent the bow digging into the waves.

AIRFLOW

The gennaker can be sheeted in tightly to lift the bow of the boat, rather than it digging into the waves.

Tighten the mainsheet to reduce twist, which decreases the leverage from the top of the sail and therefore the risk of nosediving. Additional depowering can be made by rotating the mast aft, but it is important to not go too far, as the mast can become inverted and bend.

Set the jib to its telltales, but it can be over eased to further depower.

Downwind in stronger winds with the crew even further back

TECHNIQUE

In all but the strongest of winds it's fast to have the windward hull just out of the water. The technique is to head up carefully and lock on to the apparent wind, creating a dramatic increase in speed and power. This may cause the leeward hull to dip if your timing and anticipation is wrong. At this point bear away sharply, easing the gennaker sheet as before. Once again balance and trim is everything.

The demands on the crew in these conditions are immense: keep your eyes out of the boat and communicate: have a running commentary such as: "Bearing away – ease the sheet" or "Heading up – sheet in".

If it looks as though you are going to capsize to leeward, continue to bear away until things stabilise or even until the catamaran is going straight downwind: not fast but safe. Note: by going fast, the pressure on the mainsails is reduced, making nose diving less of a problem.

You will need to make much bigger changes in course and sail trim to keep the boat upright, almost to the point of being pro-active to gusts and waves. In a gust the helmsman needs to bear away radically but smoothly or the boat will capsize. If the gennaker sheet is not controlled at the appropriate time the bow will dig in and the boat may cartwheel forwards. If the bow does dig in significantly, it is important to use the rudders to bear away and fully ease the gennaker rapidly to release all power, try to keep your weight aft and this, combined, is your best defence against a capsize. Team work is vital!

You need grip on the water to create apparent wind, but too much grip will generate a feeling of being overpowered, tripping of the bow and difficulty in bearing away, so the boards should be lifted more as you begin to feel the bow start to dig in.

TACTICS DOWNWIND

As you round the windward mark, look to make sure that you do not get trapped to leeward of another boat. Your objective is to keep high after the mark to pick up speed before bearing off, in the way described. If you have a boat to windward you could get trapped on a low course, unable to accelerate, with the only immediate option of gybing away.

Importantly beware of boats still beating up to the windward mark on port when you are bearing away on starboard. If a gust comes you will need to bear away to avoid a capsize, but the rules say that you must give the port boat opportunity to keep clear and this may just not be possible. The solution is to think further ahead.

Remember, boats are travelling fast, sailing angles are changing all the time, some boats will be sailing upwind through your course: port gives way to starboard and windward boat keeps clear!

OVERTAKING TO WINDWARD

Tactically you have the advantage, as your opponent cannot see your change in course. Concentrate on boatspeed, luffing up and bearing away as appropriate. When you are approximately abeam of your rival, choose an effective gust to bear away and drive over the top of them.

OVERTAKING TO LEEWARD

The best option, if you are running deeper and faster than your opponent, is to gybe away into clean air, although this is not always an option. Breaking through a windward boat is difficult but not impossible – by working each gust more efficiently, and using the apparent wind to sail deeper, you can produce a sufficient gap to allow you to luff up at the opportune moment and drive through.

Overtaking to windward

DOWNWIND TROUBLESHOOTING

Problem	Cause	Solution
Lack of power in the gennaker	Airflow not attached to the sail	Head up to attach airflow
Catamaran loses direction when steering	Not enough board down	Lower boards to create resistance to sideways drift
Difficulty in bearing away in gusts	Boat not balanced properly	Move crew weight aft / Check that the windward daggerboard is raised / Raise the leeward daggerboard further / Crew to ease the gennaker during the manoeuvre
Helm feels twitchy	Being overpowered	Check the twist of the mainsail leech and reduce / Lift boards / React earlier
Hull not lifting	Not sheeted in enough / Sailing too low / Boards too high	Create more power by sheeting in, heading up and / or lowering boards

Hurricane going downwind

GYBING

Downwind you are looking for greater wind pressure because more pressure means more speed, which then allows you to sail deeper. So you may need to gybe to get into greater pressure or because you have reached the layline.

The secret of gybing is to do it at speed. If you bear away and pussyfoot about, the catamaran will slow and the sails will load up and, when they do cross the cat, they will do so with a good deal of pressure behind them.

So build up maximum speed on a broad reach. As you turn into the gybe, ease the gennaker sheet until the clew is approximately half way along the jib. When you do gybe the gennaker will naturally blow through between the jib and its own luff. If you ease it too far it will wrap around its own luff and if you don't let it out far enough it can lay against the jib and have to be pulled through or possibly lead to a capsize.

Self-tacking jibs are now the norm but if you don't have one, re-setting the jib during the gybe is of secondary importance, although it's a good idea to release the sheet as you head downwind.

The helm should concentrate firstly on building up speed and secondly on making a smooth turn. After the gybe, head up to lock on to the new apparent wind before bearing away onto the proper course. Note that after a gybe in light winds you will need to come up higher to pick up good speed, while in strong winds strike a balance between speed and control – indeed if you come up too high you risk a capsize on the new gybe.

MEDIUM WINDS

As with the tack, good communication is key when gybing a performance cat.

- Find a flatter spot to gybe in.
- Continue to sail the catamaran fast for as long as possible before starting the turn.
- The crew lifts themselves on the trapeze.
- Using their non-sheet hand, the crew pulls themselves back into the boat, ideally onto their feet, while keeping the gennaker filling.
- Once the crew is on board, the helm initiates the turn, aiming for a consistent turn rate throughout the manoeuvre.
- As the stern goes through the wind, the crew picks up the new spinnaker sheet and uses that to gybe the gennaker.
- While this is happening, the helm moves onto their knees and shuffles across the boat while still holding the tiller connecting bar and mainsheet.
- As the mainsheet begins to fill on the new side, both of you should be applying your weight to the new windward side.
- Having filled the spinnaker, the crew looks for the trapeze and rolls out into the trapezing position as soon as possible.

- The helm moves back to their stable sitting position and builds power as appropriate by slowly luffing back onto the wind.

- Meanwhile the crew will have moved back and, once they are secure in the rear toe loop, the cat should be bought back to the full downwind speed.

If required, the helm can ease the mainsheet into the gybe and pull it in when coming out of the gybe to increase acceleration.

1 From the first reach

2 The crew comes in off the wire, picking up the new gennaker sheet and the helm begins to bear away

3 Go through the gybe

4 Prepare on the new gybe

5 Head up to attach the airflow to the sail

6 As the apparent wind is generated, go out on the wire and bear away

Gybing a gennaker single handed is a challenge, but you should prioritise steering, helm movement and gennaker sheeting and look to control these. The mainsheet can be left cleated and, in tension, will act as a backstay to support the mast.

LIGHT WINDS

In light winds the procedure is much the same, but if the top battens don't 'pop', a quick tug on the down-haul should make them. It might be the case that both of you are on board the cat: in this instance take care to move around the boat as smoothly as possible during the gybe, to minimise speed loss and aid acceleration.

STRONG WINDS

Much the same as medium conditions, however, when it is blowing more, the boat is moving faster and so smaller rudder movements are required to turn the boat: make the turn slower and give every-one time to go through their procedures. Make sure everything has been done and you are both ready before powering up again.

THE LEEWARD MARK

At the leeward mark you are looking to drop the gennaker, round the mark and head up onto the new beat in as efficient way as possible.

- The crew should lift themselves on the trapeze and enter the boat as with the gybe: keeping the gennaker flying.
- The helm eases the mainsheet and bears off onto a dead downwind course (which takes the load off the gennaker).
- The crew lets go of the gennaker sheet, releases the gennaker halyard and immediately starts pulling the retrieval line.
- When it is approximately half way down, the tack line needs to be released to allow the gennaker all the way into the chute.
- The helm needs to position themselves on the windward hull on their knees, facing in, with their feet locked over the edge of the hull.
- The crew puts the daggerboard down and adjusts the rig controls for the beat: rotator back to the upwind position and downhaul on as required.
- To round the buoy, the helm pushes the tiller.
- As the catamaran rounds up, both roll out onto the trapeze, with the helm sheeting in the mainsail and the crew tightening the jib as they go out.
- They lower themselves on their trapezes to their normal beating position and the crew takes the mainsheet again and makes any final adjustments to the rig controls.

1 Approaching the leeward mark, the crew comes in off the wire

2 The helm bears away and the crew starts to lower the gennaker

3 As the gennaker goes into the chute the helm heads up

4 And gets onto the wind to pass the mark

TACTICS AT THE LEEWARD MARK

If you plan to approach on port, beware: half the fleet may be coming in starboard turning into an inside overlap as you enter the 3 boat length circle. You will need to give them room to go round inside. Try to keep good speed, aiming slightly above the mark to allow for bearing away and dropping. As you bear away, the 'overlap line' closes in your favour.

If you are coming in on port and trying to get an overlap on the same tack boat ahead you can consider a late drop, but if you reach the mark with your gennaker still half up you will be penalised if you are unable to round up onto the wind and force them wide.

Arriving at the leeward mark on starboard and planning to do a gybe drop is a working tactic as room at the mark is normally established, but leave yourself a bit of room to turn and drop the gennaker. Once again, if you exit the mark with the gennaker half down and unable to come up to your proper course you will be liable to be protested.

My personal preference is to arrive near the mark on starboard and gybe about 20 lengths from it. This gives you the advantage of being on starboard for most of the way and also gives you time to do a clean gybe drop and make a smart rounding. There are laylines to the leeward mark and you need to think about where they are. Ideally you will gybe on the layline, but if you are in doubt and it's windy, gybe early to avoid having to reach to the mark. If it's light, you may choose to go past the layline, gybe late and come in to the mark higher on the wind with good speed.

Think about your tactics before you arrive at the leeward mark

REACHING

On a typical race course, you won't be reaching crosswind in a high performance cat, but there may be times when you are forced to – perhaps in handicap or long distance racing, or if the wind has swung dramatically on a standard race course.

Although reaching with the gennaker set is exhilarating, it is essentially a light-to-medium wind technique. In strong winds the catamaran may develop lots of lee helm (i.e. you have to push the tiller to keep the cat on course). Often the sideways drift created is more trouble than it's worth, and in a gust you may not be able to bear away quickly enough to prevent a capsize. With the daggerboards down (to resist drift), the catamaran can quickly lift a hull and bearing away is resisted by the foils and sail set.

MEDIUM WINDS

This normally requires twin trapezing. The skill is to play the gennaker sheet and the mainsheet continuously to keep the cat up to speed. If constantly overpowered it is more effective to pull on main downhaul rather than sheet out the mainsail too much which closes the slot between the main and the gennaker. Pulling on the downhaul twists off and flattens the top of the mainsail, which is above gennaker height.

CREW WEIGHT

The crew should be to windward, on and off the trapeze as appropriate and fore and aft as appropriate for trim and balance.

AIRFLOW

The helmsman will need to play the mainsheet and occasionally adjust the downhaul to keep the catamaran balanced and powered up. Whether you decide to play the mainsheet or the traveller will come from experience.

Set the jib to the telltales.

TECHNIQUE

Set the daggerboards such that the catamaran can create forward speed without being totally overpowered. This allows you to bear away quickly in a gust, although for good performance in slightly lighter winds you would aim to put more boards down to give maximum resistance.

In a lull, the crew simply comes in board, trimming the gennaker to the new wind. In a gust be ready to convert the generated power into forward speed by bearing away and easing the gennaker sheet to allow the cat to accelerate. Finally, come back up, without the windward hull flying too high.

If you're experiencing too much lee helm, try moving crew weight aft. If the load on the gennaker sheet is excessive, try easing the gennaker tack line – this brings the sail further aft, reducing the turning effect.

LIGHT WINDS

CREW WEIGHT

Both helm and crew should be forward, with the crew's head just to windward of the mast.

AIRFLOW

Rotate the mast until the spanner bar points at the leeward shroud. In essence the mast is not very rotated because the apparent wind is well forward. The downhaul should be just tight enough to re-move creases although, once moving, increasing downhaul tension may help. Set the traveller on the centreline.

The helmsman steers to the luff of the gennaker.

Trim the jib to the telltales, probably right in.

TECHNIQUE

The leeward daggerboard should be down, to resist the pressure to drift sideways, and the windward daggerboard should be between down and half up.

As the catamaran heads up from a broad reach, sheet in the gennaker. Eventually there comes a point where the sail is simply dragging the boat sideways, creating no forward power. It's important to identify this point, and mark the sheet where it comes through the ratchet block.

Once the sheet is trimmed (almost) to this set-ting, all the helmsman can do is to steer a course to maximise boatspeed, reacting to the apparent wind. There is no point in sheeting in harder and trying to head higher, as you will lose speed, in-crease leeway and heeling.

STRONG WINDS

CREW WEIGHT

The crew should be as far out and as far back as you can manage.

AIRFLOW

Your objective is to depower the main as much as possible. Rotate the mast so that the spanner points towards the leeward rear beam housing, and then apply full downhaul and outhaul tensions.

It is likely that, in these kind of conditions, the gennaker will provide too much power to handle on a reach, so keep it in the chute. Set the mainsail traveller in a position where the mainsheet can be managed easily by the crew.

Trim the jib so that it's not really doing anything, but is not flapping.

TECHNIQUE

Put the daggerboards in a position where the boat is not too overpowered; for less power lift the boards further.

Normally you wouldn't carry a gennaker on a strong wind reach, but you may find that you are forced to do this if the conditions change, As with all gennaker sailing, you need to steer a course that gives you space to leeward to bear away into when you need it. The skill of strong wind gennaker reaching is to keep the speed up (which takes the pressure off the rig) and to be able to depower the rig substantially.

In a gust bear away hard and keep going until the speed has built up and you can recover your original direction.

Again, if you need to bear away, do so rapidly and make sure that the crew eases the sheet as you do.

PART 3

143

TACTICS ON A REACH

If you can lay the next mark under the gennaker, hoist and go!

If you can't lay the mark because it is set too high you have two choices:

- EITHER sail high initially, hoist and reach to the next mark.
- OR hoist immediately, forcing you to sail low and below the next mark, then drop and close reach to the mark before gybing and hoisting again on the next leg.

All things being equal the first option is the best as you are only required to hoist once and you are more likely to keep clear air during the first leg.

OVERTAKING TO WINDWARD

If you are overtaking to windward, take care, because you will not be able to bear away in a gust. Similarly, be very careful about passing close to windward of somebody who is not flying a gennaker: if they luff, you are obliged to respond. Keep a good distance to weather and at the opportune moment bear away in a gust.

OVERTAKING TO LEEWARD

Passing to leeward is difficult without a sufficient gap below other boats to maintain some stability in the wind. Be more ready to bear off in a gust than your opponent, break through and then slowly regain the windward ground you have lost.

REACHING TROUBLESHOOTING

Problem	Cause	Solution
Catamaran trips up bearing away in a gust	Daggerboard providing too much grip	Raise the leeward daggerboard slightly
Mainsail needs excessive adjustment	Mainsail too full	Pull on more downhaul
Catamaran capsizes across the wind	Overpowered / helm too slow to bear away	Bear away earlier to generate forward power
Gennaker keeps collapsing	Gennaker too full / sailing too close to the wind	Check luff tension, or sail a lower course
Unable to maintain required course	Too much power in the sails	Bear away and drop the gennaker
Mainsail flogging ineffectively / starts to 'pant'	Mainsheet overeased	Bear away and drop the gennaker
Catamaran sails sideways	Lack of grip	Bear away / ease gennaker Create forward movement and lift from the daggerboards before luffing up
Gennaker does not curl	Gennaker too flat	Release halyard tension slightly so head falls away from mast (use this if trying to make a mark)
Leeward helm	Centre of effort too far forward	Ease gennaker and power up the mainsail

There are a few basic checks you should carry out before stepping the mast. Check that:

- The mast is straight.
- The spreaders are aligned and evenly deflected.
- The diamond wires are the right length (you can also use the diamonds to straighten a bent mast) – as a starting point, their tension should be 40 on the Loos Gauge with the spreaders perfectly horizontal to the mast.
- The pulleys are running smoothly and the halyard lock mechanisms are working.

Once stepped, mast tuning is a 3D puzzle. The mast can bend sideways, fore-and-aft or along its axis. The shape and stability of the mast are determined by numerous elements: the mast rake, rig tension, diamonds, spreaders, downhaul tension, mast rotation and mainsheet tension. These work together through the sail and mast to increase or decrease the power.

There are so many variations possible that you really need to record your different set ups and how they perform so that you can either repeat them easily or avoid them! To do this you will need a straight edge and rule to measure the spreader rake and a rig tension gauge (Loos Gauge) to measure the diamond and rig tension. Your class rigging manual should provide settings to allow you to get reasonable settings straightaway.

To really understand your rig, you need to spend time watching and feeling it react. This is best done on the shore with the catamaran secured and on the water from a support boat observing and taking pictures. Finally there is nothing quite as useful as testing setups against another cat through two-boat tuning.

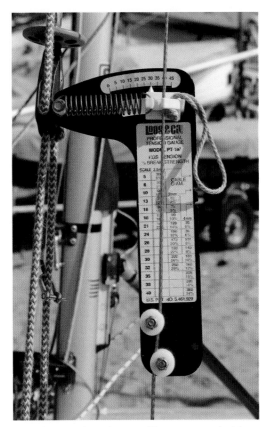

Measure your settings and tensions and keep a record of them

MAST RAKE

The mast rake is determined by the forestay / jib halyard length. It would tend to be raked back in stronger conditions and be more upright when lighter.

The rake of the mast also affects the location of the centre of effort in the mainsail, which should ideally be directly above the centre of lateral resistance from the daggerboard.

RIG TENSION

The rig tension is controlled by the shroud length. Obviously, both shrouds need to be the same length, so the mast is upright.

In lighter winds, there needs to be more give in the rig and so you will set the rig tension looser – typically 25-30 on the Loos Gauge. As the wind gets up, you increase the rig tension: it keeps tension on the forestay even when you've eased the mainsheet, keeping the mainsail flatter for longer.

Usually you are not allowed to adjust the shroud length during a race.

DIAMONDS

The diamonds support about two-thirds of the mast. The rigidity of this part of the mast depends on the tension in the diamond wires, the length of the spreaders and the angle at which they sweep back.

So, a light crew may need more pre-bend in strong winds to permanently flatten the mainsail. This is achieved by sweeping back the spreaders and increasing the tension in the diamond wires. In light winds by decreasing the tension, and hence the pre-bend, more power can be reintroduced.

As mentioned above, start from a tension of 40 on the Loos Gauge: tighter in strong winds and looser in light winds. However, if the tension is too low (and the windward diamond wire goes slack), the mast is bending sideways excessively and is not supported well enough – tighten the diamonds up until this does not happen. If in doubt, tension up the diamond wires to create positive pre-bend.

Note: Excessive sweeping back of spreaders or reducing diamond tension can lead to the centre section of the mast becoming unstable, in this instance it could invert and bend into the jib slot causing loss of power / performance or even mast failure.

SPREADERS

Initially set the spreaders level with each other and evenly deflected. Place a straight edge across the back of the spreaders and measure the distance to the trailing edge of the mast.

In stronger winds, you need to depower, so angle the spreaders further back (increasing the distance to the mast) to give more pre-bend.

In lighter winds you need more power, so angle the spreaders further forward (decreasing the distance to the mast) which, in turn, gives less pre-bend.

MAINSAIL DOWNHAUL

The downhaul dramatically changes the shape of the mainsail. It is your first dynamic control when racing. By applying tension you attempt to stretch the sails luff length, compressing the mast and bending it across its axis from the top to the base. The effect is to flatten the sail and open the top third of the leech: an excellent tool for strong upwind sailing. You need to practice using the downhaul effectively, smoothly and in coordination with the rest of the boat's equipment.

In one sense the downhaul is the fine tuning of the diamond wire settings, allowing you to increase and decrease power over a limited range. It also has implications on the foot of the sail (see section on the outhaul).

The control can be operated by the crew or the helm (depending on who is working the mainsheet), easing the downhaul for power and applying tension when the catamaran feels overpowered or requires large amounts of mainsheet adjustment.

Downwind the downhaul needs to be eased to decrease the mast bend. There is a danger that the extra load created by the gennaker, with the mast being bent by the downhaul tension, will cause a mast failure.

MAST ROTATION

The initial purpose of allowing the mast to rotate is to give a smoother airflow over the leeward side of the mainsail. Effectively this means pointing the leeward side towards the direction of the apparent wind.

A second effect is mast bend. When downhaul or mainsheet tension is applied there is a pull down on the luff or the leech. By adjusting rotation you increase or decrease how the mast responds to the tensions applied. The basic principle is that the more the mast is rotated across the cat the more power, and the more the mast is de-rotated and points towards the rear beam the less power is generated because the top of the mast bends off to leeward.

A good basic rule is to point the mast towards the shroud plate for light and medium winds, moving it towards the rear beam housing as the wind increases. But don't do this too early as too much de-rotation will result in the top of the mast bending off to leeward, above the hounds, giving reduced performance and making the rig unstable.

MAINSHEET TENSION

The mainsheet also controls sail twist and the bend in the mast tip.

Increasing mainsheet tension reduces twist, and the resulting leech tension will also bend the top of the mast aft, the exact amount depending on mast rotation.

Upwind the mainsheet should be as tight as possible. Downwind it needs to be eased to tie in with the apparent wind direction, although it remains relatively tight. It needs to be played constantly to keep the sail working efficiently.

OTHER MAINSAIL CONTROLS

While the above controls have a significant effect on the mast, as well as other aspects of performance, there are also lots of other controls to consider.

MAINSAIL OUTHAUL

The mainsail outhaul adjusts the tension on the foot of the sail. In lighter winds you are looking for a deeper, fuller sail (looser outhaul) and in stronger winds you want a flatter sail (tighter outhaul).

However, as mentioned earlier, the downhaul also has an effect: pulling on it shortens the foot and when you release the downhaul you will notice more shape is automatically created in the foot. Set the downhaul first and then adjust the outhaul as required.

TRAVELLER

The traveller controls the angle to the mainsheet. Upwind it should generally be set in the middle of the cat until you are struggling to keep the working range on the mainsheet. The crew will be on the wire playing the mainsheet to keep the windward hull just flying. If the adjustments required are too big you need to start moving the traveller. When this happens, drop it marginally, about 50 mm at a time, until you can keep the working range of the mainsheet.

Downwind the traveller will be set in the centre, to maintain control over the top of the mast and rig.

BATTENS

Performance catamarans use tapered battens to further enhance performance. The more tension in the battens the more the sail will hold its shape and support the leech and the better it is suited to moderate winds. With less tension, the sail is easier to flatten and better suited to strong winds where too much power can be generated or light winds where too much camber can prevent the airflow from passing across the sail.

The long battens at the bottom of the mainsail just stabilise the sail, but the ones towards the top have more effect on the shape of the sail and should be adjusted as required:

- In strong winds you want to flatten off the top of the mainsail, so use stiff battens, put in loosely (just taking the wrinkles out).
- In lighter winds you want to induce belly into the sail to create power, so use softer battens and put them in firmly to increase curvature (but not too firmly to hook the sail).

Beware that battens put in firmly may be hard to pop in tacking and gybing manoeuvres.

JIB CONTROLS

JIB LUFF

The jib luff control mirrors the mainsail downhaul:

- To reduce power: tighten it, this drags the draft forward and flattens the sail.
- To increase power: loosen it, bringing fullness into the sail (but avoid any sagging or scalloping).

JIB CLEWBOARD

The clewboard allows you to adjust the vertical angle of the jibsheet:

- In strong winds you need a shallow angle (lower on the clewboard) so that the foot of the jib is in tension and there is some twist in the leech.
- In lighter winds, go higher on the clewboard to create power, but be careful not to hook the leech of the jib.

JIB CAR

This adjusts the horizontal angle of the jibsheet:

- In strong winds: ease it out to feather the jib slightly: it should mirror the mainsail traveller.
- In lighter winds: move it towards the middle to create more power, but be careful not to bring it in too far and close the slot between the mainsail and jib too much.

JIBSHEET

This is the over-riding jib control: it provides your first point of call when adjusting the sail while sailing. Provided the other jib controls are roughly in position, the sheet will be used when the boat changes from one course to another, or if the wind strength changes dramatically. Mirroring what the mainsheet does, the jibsheet should be tighter on an upwind course, and then loosened when sailing off the wind. Keep an eye on the gap between the mainsail and jib (the slot) and try to keep it open and parallel.

DAGGERBOARDS

The daggerboards provide resistance from slipping sideways when required.

Upwind, they should be down to provide grip and lateral resistance. As the wind increases, when you are struggling to hold the cat down and losing forward drive, you should begin to bring the daggerboards up.

Downwind, it is a balance:

- Since high performance catamarans have the potential of going faster than the wind downwind, the daggerboards have the potential to create flow rather than the catamaran just being blown downwind.
- But they can cause some drag which you want to avoid.

Have them about 50% up to provide some lateral resistance and to lift the hull, but to minimise the drag they cause. Potentially, in lighter winds they might go further down to help lift the hull earlier. If the boat is beginning to trip over itself, then they should come up a bit further.

Downwind have the daggerboards about 50% up

PART 4
NEW DEVELOPMENTS

FOILING & WING SAILS

While really outside the scope of this book, in this final section we take a glimpse at the exciting developments in catamarans through the eyes of co-author Tom Phipps:

As a high performance catamaran sailor I have been very fortunate that, during my sailing career, production sailing catamarans have developed hugely. Advances in build materials, manufacturing processes and an added America's Cup incentive have pushed catamarans into overdrive. Like Formula 1 car racing, ideas from the high budget world of the America's Cup filter their way down to the smaller boats and eventually into the production market.

Foiling isn't a new idea, and in fact many might say that we are decades late after projects like the 'Icarus' foiling Tornado (in the 1970s). However it's only in recent years that materials and manufacturing processes have caught up with the load requirements of such boats and today the sky is literally the limit.

My personal experience of foiling has been a stepped process. The introduction of C-Foils and the Nacra 17 as the Olympic Class catamaran for 2012 was the first time I experienced the effect of how reduced displacement kicked a boat into another gear. While not fully foiling for the 2016 Olympics, the catamaran used a C-Foil that curved in under the platform to provide an element of vertical lift. This reduces the effective weight of the boat in the water and substantially decreases the drag.

The concept not only boosts a boat's stable sailing performance; the additional lift also contributes to the age-old catamaran problem of the inevitable nose dive and pitchpole during downwind legs. Vertical lift at that position in the boat helps lift the bow and, in fact, at high speeds it can often not be a case of nose div-

C-Foils provide lift, but are not fully foiling

ing, but stopping the boat trying to go into orbit riding due to excessive vertical lift in the bow section. Quick and accurate crew weight movement is required to monitor the boat's trim and foil's pitch angle to keep her stable and sailing smoothly.

The next step for me, in the hydro foiling process, was 'full take-off'. The design and concept of this type of catamaran can be very closely linked to the latest America's Cup (AC) style catamarans. There are a number of foil options when you get to this stage of design. As ever with design there will always be trade-off and ongoing developments: the consideration here is the balance between efficiency and stability. For instance, a wand system (with T-Foils), much the same as seen on the International Moth, is stable but, when installed on a larger catamaran, the foils required are bigger and with two on each hull, the drag is increased and therefore the platform's performance is limited.

In contrast, and from my biggest experience of catamaran foiling, the J-Foil – similar to those used on the recent AC cats – is a very efficient foil shape, and allows the boat to reach extremely high speeds but, in the unstable world of racing on water, the foil is more susceptible to stalling. Foils like these on the larger boats use an element of electrical computer systems to prevent them from stalling. Naturally, in the smaller boats that luxury isn't quite as appropriate, and so it becomes a challenge for the crew to keep solid stable flow over the foil. In addition, for a dynamic crew, there is also a control to adjust the pitch angle of the foil which dictates how much lift the foil will create.

However, as before, there is another compromise: increased lift also increases the foil's drag and limits its terminal speed forward. For that reason, on board the platform we have 2 distinct pitch angles and modes. In 'Take off' mode, the foil is set with a large amount of lift. As the boat begins to foil and accelerate we change the foil into 'Foiling' mode where the drag is reduced allowing the platform to continue to accelerate. This is a progressive control and one that takes time to master.

Having spent some time sailing the J-Foil Flying Phantom, it is clear that, without hydraulic and electronic controls, manoeuvring the boats on the foils is a challenge. The need to lift and lower the windward foil from tack to tack gives the crew a huge amount of jobs to check off as they cross the boat. Accurate foil set up is key as the boat transitions from one foil in the water in a straight line, to two through the middle of the tack and then back to one on the exit.

J-Foils lift you right out of the water, but require significant and dynamic adjustment to get the best out of them

With the decision in November 2016 to move the Nacra 17 to a fully foiling catamaran for the 2020 Olympics it is clear that a new era of foiling catamarans is opening up and one in which I very much look forward to being part of. After installing the newly developed Z-Foil we were asked to sail the prototype boat prior to the decision and can't wait to have our own boat to start practising on!

Another notable point, when moving from a traditional multihull to a foiling platform, is how the use of the gennaker changes. In solid foiling conditions, what used to be the deep downwind engine on traditional cats becomes redundant. On a downwind course the extra speed from foiling moves the apparent wind on the boat so far forward that it becomes impossible to flatten the gennaker enough to prevent it from collapsing, in which case the sail becomes a burden on the platform's speed and thus higher efficiency is achieved without it. However, as a caveat, in very light winds the gennaker can provide the extra power to foil earlier, and in very strong winds can be used to actually slow the boat for more control while on the foil. After all, a boat upside down is slower that any mode upright!

Another recent explosion in the high performance catamaran world is the use of solid wings as an alternative to the traditional soft sail and mast combination. My experience of this came from my time spent with the British C Class catamaran project 'Invictus'. There is solid fact behind the knowledge that there is more power created by a wing sail than a soft sail: this is demonstrated no better than in the case of the C Class catamarans. There is no word that I know of that can describe the feeling of being fully powered up, flat out on the trapeze in what is next to no wind using a solid wing.

However, all this additional performance comes at a cost, not only to the wallet but practically as well. Having been part of the wing build with Team Invictus I know that the internal systems to control such a powerful machine are not only intricate but numerous to say the least. Most wings are bespoke and, therefore, all a little different.

In the case of the Invictus wing, there were three primary controls, sheet, camber and twist:
- Sheet was the most active control and acted like a mainsheet on a conventional sail: by adjusting the angle of the elements to the wind, we were able to control the majority of power the wing produced.

No words can describe the sensation of being on the trapeze with a fully powered up wing sail

There is a small working window when the wind becomes an incredible machine

- *Camber changed the amount the middle of the wing fell away: in essence the depth of a soft sail.*
- *The twist function allowed the top of the wing to blade off, in the same way a downhaul system affects a traditional sail.*

Between these three controls the huge wing is actually very controllable: power can be produced and released accurately and efficiently. One thing I particularly noticed whilst sailing with a wing is the narrow performance groove in which a wing works. While on a soft sail you can have half the sail back winding and the other half working, a wing is either on or off. There is a small working window when the wing becomes an incredible machine, outside of that it's stalled and next to useless.

Lastly, and probably the biggest reason, we will not be seeing solid wing sails on production catamarans immediately, is the practical challenges that come with them. Storage, assembly and rigging are all areas where things take time and space. During the C Class championship hosted by Windsport, 10 boats competed and the space needed was vast. However for development, exhibition and prestigious events, such as the C Class championships and the America's Cup, wings are no doubt the weapon of choice. They provide designers with a mountain of technical options and challenges. Perhaps in the future, as with foils, these beautiful engineering masterpieces will make their way into the production market, but for now it will still be battens and halyards.

Tom Phipps

www.tomphippsracing.co.uk

ACKNOWLEDGEMENTS

Few books are the product of just one person's achievements and our thanks must go to all the sailors and Windsport coaches that we have worked with who have contributed to the development of the systems we now use. The Windsport team on the water or in the office are all contributors: we thank them all.

We also wish to thank two catamaran sailors who in their time have made a valuable contribution to catamaran sailing worldwide and our own personal catamaran sailing over the years and this book: thank you Kim Stephens and Ian Fraser.

Tom and Brian Phipps
Windsport Catamaran Coaching

*For up-to-date information about catamaran class associations and useful links about catamaran sailing, please visit: **www.fernhurstbooks.com/other-resources/catamarans***